Child Abuse and
the Social Environment

Child Abuse and
the Social Environment

George E. Fryer, Jr.

Westview Press

BOULDER • SAN FRANCISCO • OXFORD

This Westview softcover edition is printed on acid-free paper and bound in library-quality, coated covers that carry the highest rating of the National Association of State Textbook Administrators, in consultation with the Association of American Publishers and the Book Manufacturers' Institute.

Published in 1993 in the United States of America by Westview Press, Inc., 5500 Central Avenue, Boulder, Colorado 80301-2877, and in the United Kingdom by Westview Press, 36 Lonsdale Road, Summertown, Oxford OX2 7EW

A CIP catalog record for this book is available from the Library of Congress.
ISBN 0-8133-1803-3

Printed and bound in the United States of America

The paper used in this publication meets the requirements
of the American National Standard for Permanence of Paper
for Printed Library Materials Z39.48-1984.

10   9   8   7   6   5   4   3   2   1

In memory of Katie Fryer,

my granddaughter

Contents

Tables and Figures

Tables

Figures

Foreword

The future of a country lies with its children. While being a continuing resource, they require nurturing in order to develop to the point where they can benefit a country. If nurturing is absent or inadequate, children are unlikely to realize full potential. In some instances they may die in their infancy or childhood, long before they have had an opportunity to explore their potential. This book suggests that what we are doing to protect and nurture this most important resource is woefully inadequate.

The last decade has witnessed a startling increase in the number of cases of suspected child maltreatment. However, the lack of a scientifically based national surveillance system prevents us from knowing the actual magnitude of the problem. What is known is devastating. When child maltreatment occurs, the developmental and emotional effects frequently extend into the adult years where another cycle of maltreatment too often is initiated. In one sense, however, these victims are fortunate; at least they had some opportunity to recover--there are many children who die early in life as a result of maltreatment.

As one reads the book, a number of emotions are experienced. An initial emotion is surprise--especially surprise at the extent of the problem. Sadness is experienced as one realizes the devastating effects of maltreatment on the child victims, their families and their friends. One becomes frustrated when, over and over again, the critical areas of knowledge needed to address the problem are missing. But the most overwhelming reaction is anger--anger because our resolve as a nation to solve this problem is weak, some would even say lacking. We spend millions of dollars trying to ensure that all pregnant girls and women receive adequate prenatal care. This is money well spent. But almost nothing is spent on teenage pregnancy programs, an issue central to child maltreatment, since teenage mothers are disproportionately represented among the population that is involved in maltreatment cases. We spend millions of dollars studying the etiology of the disease and problems of childhood and adolescence, i.e., childhood cancer, juvenile diabetes, asthma, substance abuse and learning disorders. This is money well spent. Precious little is spent on efforts to understand the etiology of child maltreatment, despite the fact that child maltreatment is probably an important factor in the etiology of many adolescent problems such as depression, drug abuse and suicide. We spend millions of dollars on efficacy and effectiveness studies of interventions to improve the health of school age children and youth. There have been literally hundreds of studies addressing such issues as cigarette smoking, alcohol use, nutrition, fitness and depression among this population. This is money well spent, but few studies have assessed the effects of child maltreatment prevention programs. The national commitment seen in the other areas to develop and experimentally assess innovative prevention and intervention programs is lacking in the area of child maltreatment. Too often what is known about the prevention and intervention of child maltreatment is not widely disseminated. The system charged with the authority and responsibility to protect the infants and children and help the families too often seems to be inefficient, ineffective and unresponsive. The feeling of anger lingers as one starts to read about the details of the study reported herein.

This study addresses a series of questions using a large database--data on 33 variables for 944 counties in 18 states. A number of important findings emerge from the analyses: Child maltreatment is found in all counties, regardless of their population; Black, Hispanic and Caucasian children are victimized; the vast majority of maltreatment occurs within the family unit; and a state's reporting and follow-up procedures influence the extent to which the actual problem is identified. The study's results reenforce what has been suspected, i.e., that family structure has a profound influence on the occurrence of physical abuse, and family economic status has a profound influence on child neglect. Counties with high and low rates of child maltreatment were identified with uncanny accuracy, thus providing an immediate opportunity for case-finding activities at the county level. Perhaps the most important finding, however, is what wasn't found--using 33 environmental variables, only 34 percent of the variance of county-level child maltreatment rates could be explained. Clearly, we have much to learn.

If, as a nation, we are committed to preventing child maltreatment: when it occurs, identify the case and intervene immediately; there is much we need to do now. A national system to identify and manage child maltreatment cases must be established and maintained. There should be little variance in the implementation of the system at the state level. The county and state level systems that have been assigned responsibility for child maltreatment should be examined from a 'zero-based budgeting' perspective, i.e., assume that nothing is sacred and everything must be justified. There needs to be a significant and continuing commitment to research child maltreatment-- studies on the etiology of maltreatment, studies on the efficacy and effectiveness of prevention and intervention programs and studies on the diffusion of successful programs are needed. As Fryer points out, there is an urgent need to assemble data sets that are suitable for secondary data analyses. If the child maltreatment problem is to be significantly reduced, as a nation we must resolve to address the social issues that Fryer and others have noted underlie much of the problem--notably, the economic status of families, the eroding family structure and reduced educational opportunities. This represents the most immediate challenge as we prepare to enter the 21st century.

Ed Fryer is to be commended for assembling the data in this book. He makes a compelling argument about the need to take immediate action on many fronts. More importantly, the data and his text capture our interest at a very personal level. Hopefully, his efforts in writing this book will help to produce the dividend we all await--the prevention of child maltreatment and the creation of a society that really cares about its most valuable resource--our children.

Donald C. Iverson, Ph.D.
Professor and Vice Chairman
  of Research and Academic Affairs
Health Sciences Center
University of Colorado
Denver, Colorado

Acknowledgments

Many scholars and professionals dedicated to the protection of children and service to the members of their families have contributed to development of the ideas put forth in this book. I am grateful to them all. But to some, I am especially indebted. Drs. Merle Adams, Herb Bynder, Ray Cuzzort, Bob Hunter and Jules Wanderer gave unsparingly of themselves in this effort. Each brought valuable insights to my work and I shall always be grateful for their guidance. John Fluke generously gave his time and wisdom providing child maltreatment data for my use and explaining both its value and limitations. I am thankful to Ann Underwood for her help in completing this manuscript. She gave friendship and the steady encouragement I needed to complete this task.

G.E.F.

1

Introduction

Dr. C. Henry Kempe introduced 'the battered child syndrome' in the early 1960s as the first medical diagnosis for child maltreatment. Thereafter, public understanding and interest in child abuse has soared, momentum has built for the development and implementation of protection programs, and professionals from a variety of disciplines have been trained to serve victims of abuse. While abuse and neglect of children had been known for centuries, it was Dr. Kempe's publication that galvanized states and communities to recognize the problem and begin to do something about it.

Kempe (1962) in his famous article published in the *Journal of the American Medical Association,* coauthored with several physician associates, reported the results of a nationwide study of child abuse cases. The authors cited a disinclination on the part of physicians to explore the possibility of parental maltreatment of children and the serious physical injury and death of children caused by abuse. A model child abuse reporting law was soon drafted, and by 1967 every state in the country had adopted legislation requiring specified professionals to report suspected and known cases of child maltreatment and awarding reporters immunity from liability for their action. Paulsen (1966) observed that widespread adoption of these laws had taken place in a remarkably short period of time.

Regrettably, legislative bodies have been more willing to formulate and enact laws requiring reporting of child maltreatment than to allocate monies for the handling of reported cases. Paulsen (1966) has argued that the good intentions of child protection laws require that communities develop multidisciplinary teams to ensure that something is done each time a report of child maltreatment is made. Meaningful action must be taken in response to public and professional reports of abuse or neglect which are made in good faith. For example, the number of cases of suspected child abuse and neglect reported to departments of social service in the last ten years has increased several fold. Yet, foster care capacity, the provision for out-of-home placement of children in need of protection, has remained constant in most states during that same period.

Because of the lack of systematic knowledge of the extent of child abuse in this country at the time, a major survey was administered by NORC in

1965. A national quota sample of 1,520 adult Americans was selected on the basis of age, sex, race, and employment status. This survey demonstrated a surprising propensity among the general population to abuse a child:

1. 58.3 percent of all respondents expressed the opinion that "almost anybody could at some time injure a child in his care."
2. 22.3 percent of all respondents believed "he could at some time injure a child."
3. 15.9 percent of all respondents admitted that "at one time he could hardly refrain from injuring a child in his care." (p. 55)

Gil (1970) considered admission of having nearly actually abused a child for whom one was caring extremely difficult and regarded the survey estimate of the proportion of the adult population who had injured a child as conservative. The reluctance of survey participants to concede having had thoughts or taken actions which are socially undesirable has been documented (Sudman & Bradburn, 1986).

A nationwide survey (Gil, 1970), which included every report of physical child abuse during a two-year period, paved the way for large-scale epidemiological study of the problem. These comprehensive projects usually employed representative samples. The information provided much more insight into the phenomenon of child maltreatment in the United States than the anecdotal evidence acquired from previous clinical case studies. It revealed the scope of the problem to be much greater than previously believed.

The actual incidence and prevalence of child maltreatment cannot of course be precisely determined since many cases are not brought to the attention of professionals mandated to report them. But the American Humane Association began in 1974 to collect from state departments of social service all reports of child maltreatment in an effort to determine the nature and extent of abuse and neglect in the United States. The American Humane Association estimated that in 1986 more than 2 million children were mistreated.

The epidemic had reached such brutal proportions in the 1970s that some observers asked if Americans really like children. Kenniston (1979) contends that this country's comparatively high infant mortality rate and widespread malnutrition among its children do reflect dispassionate sentiment toward them. Parental capacity to inflict pain and misery on society's youngest and most defenseless members has left many confused and bewildered. Elmer (1981) stated:

Abuse from a parent or other caretaker must be one of the most hurtful of all insults, because it combines physical pain with the psychological blow of being attacked by one's protector. The child has no way of judging the meaning of what is happening. (p. 185)

Kelly (1983) has enumerated reasons for the intense public interest in the problem of child abuse. First, professional response to child maltreatment has been genuinely multidisciplinary. Physicians, social workers, psychologists and others have been involved in both detection and treatment. More recently the legal profession has become meaningfully embroiled in the issue, as society attempts to strike a balance between the maintenance of parental rights and the protection of children.

Secondly, violence to children constitutes perhaps the most distasteful of all forms of family dysfunction. It elicits an emotional response from many professionals with case responsibility as well as members of the general public. And its consequences can be particularly severe.

Finally, the inability to gain useful insights into the etiology of the problem has been a source of frustration to scholars, practitioners and lay persons. It is difficult to understand just what possesses an individual who perpetrates such a heinous act. The members of society struggle to come to grips with behavior so incongruent with the most fundamental principles of interpersonal relations and so offensive to human sensibility.

Interest in the phenomenon of child abuse in the United States has also been fueled by sensational media reports. These reports usually involve just one or a few isolated cases. And because mistreatment of children is emotionally upsetting to even specialists who must respond clinically, sometimes inaccurate and exaggerated accounts are provided which are misleading concerning the nature and dimensions of the problem. These reports are not useful to policy makers or practitioners, although they typically arouse the public to demand action.

A huge body of clinical and scientific research findings also attest to the devastating effects of adult maltreatment of children. Sequelae documented by study results include sexual maladjustment (Bagley, 1984; Becker et al., 1986; Borgman, 1984; Brunngraber, 1986; Burgess, 1985; Cavaiola & Schiff, 1986; Coons, 1986; Cupoli, 1984; Daugherty, 1986; Finkelhor & Browne, 1986, 1985; Harcourt, 1986; Jacobsen, 1986; Johnson & Shrier, 1985; Jones, 1984; Leehan & Wilson, 1985; Maller, 1984; McCormack, Burgess & Janus, 1986; Monopolis & Sarles, 1985; Nash & West, 1985; Runtz & Briere, 1986; Stuart & Allen, 1984; Summit, 1985; Thomas & Rogers, 1984) including commission of rape, prostitution, promiscuity, indiscrete masturbatory activity, precocious sexual interest and nonorganic sexual dysfunction. Other studies have reported the deviant behavior of former victims (Anderson et al., 1983; Bagley, 1984; Becker et al., 1986; Blake-White & Kline, 1985; Borgman, 1984; Briere & Runtz, 1987; Burgess, 1986; Cavaiola & Schiff, 1986; Coons, 1986; Cupoli, 1984; Daugherty, 1984; Deighton & McPeek,

4

1985; Feldman, Mallouh & Lewis, 1986; Finkelhor & Browne, 1986; Fontana, 1984; Freeman-Longo, 1986; Garbarino, 1984; Garbarino & Plantz, 1984; Harcourt, 1986; Jacobsen, 1986; Jaffe, et al., 1986; Janus, Burgess & McCormack, 1987; Jason, 1983; Jones, 1984; Korbin, 1986; Lewis et al., 1985; McCormack, Burgess, & Janus, 1986; Middleton, 1984; Mones, 1985; Monopolis & Sarles, 1985; Mouzakitis, 1984; Oliver, 1985; Putnam & Stein, 1985; Runtz & Briere, 1986; Sandberg, 1986; Steele, 1986; Stuart & Allen, 1984; Wolfgang, 1982) such as running away from home, juvenile delinquency, substance abuse, self-mutilation and suicide attempts, mistreatment of their own children (some of which resulted in fatality), parricide and other murders, and other crimes of violence.

The above behaviors signal trouble for society. Its members must enforce the laws which are violated by certain of these acts and make provision to respond to other behaviors offensive to the community at large. For some of the more distasteful actions enumerated above, society will have little sympathy if it is not known that they stem from the actor's victimization as a child. And even when the cause of the abnormal behavior is known, the associated stigma may be damaging and enduring. Yet there are emotional and physical scars that result from brutality against children for which society collectively must make no accommodation nor pay any price beyond the quiet, sometimes unnoticed, suffering of the victim which can last a lifetime.

Many of the indications of physical maltreatment are transient: e.g., bruises, abrasions or minor burns. Forensic considerations weigh heavily in the medical diagnoses awarded by physicians with specialties in emergency medicine and general pediatrics who usually attend medically to these conditions. Their judgment of whether the injury was intentionally inflicted by an adult or the result of an accident can be crucial to the future safety of the child and to the structure and dynamics of the family.

But some of the physical consequences of child maltreatment are neither minor in severity, nor temporal in the duration of the resulting impairment. Death of the child is the most publicized outcome and is no longer viewed as a rare event (Anderson et al., 1983; Jason, 1983; Krugman, 1985; Wolfgang, 1982). More than 1,000 children are known to have been the victims in cases of murder and non-negligent manslaughter in each of the last five years (National Committee for Prevention of Child Abuse, 1989). Both abuse and neglect have been implicated in these crimes (Anderson et al., 1983) and the families of many of the deceased children were among the active caseloads of child protection agencies.

Child maltreatment has been identified as an antecedent or the causal agent of virtually every emotional and developmental impairment known to the fields of mental health and child development. Those sequelae are enumerated in Appendix A. Its content bears unmistakable witness to the severity and variety of the psychological problems that plague the victims of child abuse and neglect. It is this emotional dimension of the aftermath of child mistreatment which has overwhelmed the capacity of health and social service resources allocated to respond to the needs of abusive families.

The study presented in this book examines the need to emphasize the influence of the environment in allocating precious child protection resources, however inadequate they may be, and in responding clinically to the needs of abusive families. These problems are fully discussed in later chapters. The study also documents the utility of the ecological method, a technique appropriate to large-scale environmental study in the analysis of child maltreatment issues.

The Role of Environmental Forces

In an effort to better understand the etiology of this problem, researchers have begun to shift their focus from the behaviors and mental state of abusive parents to social forces to which they are subjected. Attention is now directed toward ecological considerations--the interaction of adult perpetrators with their environment. The social milieu in which their abusive behaviors are bred and fostered has increasingly become the substance of analyses undertaken in recent years.

The term 'stressor' has been used to represent environmental conditions which elicit stressful behavior (Blake, 1988; Kasl, 1984). The 'social stressor' was the principal element in what Gil (1979) termed the 'triggering context' in which children are mistreated. Socioeconomic pressures are the most studied among these phenomena, but elements of modern family structure (e.g., large numbers of children and single parents) have also received considerable attention from social scientists investigating the antecedents of child maltreatment. Environmental forces which focus pressure on the perpetrator of abuse lead to high rates of abuse and neglect in areas in which they are particularly prevalent. Gil (1979) viewed psychological frustration of the abusive parent as the direct result of prolonged exposure to social stressors. It follows that

the battered baby syndrome, and other forms of child abuse associated with psychological disturbances of one kind or another, are not independent of societal forces, although the perpetrators of these acts may be emotionally ill individuals. (Gil, 1979, p. 14)

In fact, alienating qualities of the environment must be seen as a logical explanation for abuse in cases in which perpetrator psychopathology cannot be traced to genetics or biochemical factors. The context in which abuse occurs is shaped by the aggregate of life experiences of the parent and child, experiences dictated largely by the social setting in which they took place (Gil, 1979).

The Application of the Ecological Method

The ecological method was originally devised to examine the context in which significant events occur and to identify possible social determinants of their occurrence. This method was modified to evaluate the role of social phenomena in child maltreatment in the study described in this book.

The environmental correlates of child maltreatment within county populations which are typical products of ecological study were supplemented with information from the individual records of abusive and neglectful families. The primary objective of this analysis was to measure the strength of association between 33 environmental variables and rates of child abuse and neglect. Data for physical abuse, sexual abuse and child neglect during 1980 were reported to the American Humane Association by 18 state departments of social services. Rates of maltreatment for the 944 counties located in those states were correlated with 33 environmental variables taken from the Area Resource File. Most were products of the 1980 national decennial census. All of the four major U.S. Bureau of the Census geographic regions were substantially represented with at least three states located in each region.

Northeast	*North Central*	*South*	*West*
Maine	Indiana	Arkansas	Arizona
New York	Michigan	Lousiana	Hawaii
Rhode Island	Minnesota	South Carolina	Nevada
Vermont	Missouri		New Mexico
	Nebraska		
	North Dakota		
	Wisconsin		

Operational definitions for child maltreatment data presented in this discussion are detailed in Technical Report #3 of the American Humane Association's *The National Study on Child Neglect and Abuse Reporting Volume 1: User Documentation* prepared by the Social System Research and Evaluation Division of the Denver Research Institute (1981). When states used a different scheme of classification for an item, the American Humane Association mapped that state's information into the most appropriate of its established National Study Data Base categories.

Within the field of child protection there is general consensus regarding the basic definitions of the most prevalent forms of child maltreatment, although the articulation of these definitions in legal statutes governing adjudication of abuse and neglect cases varies markedly from state to state. Nonetheless, formal professional definitions do enable distinctions to be made which indicate aspects of maltreatment such as the severity of its consequences. The American Humane Association definition of physical abuse has been divided into that resulting in major vs. minor physical injury. Its basis is the risk to the life and well-being of the child due to its victimization. When that risk is evaluated to be substantial, the physical injury is considered a major one. "Brain damage/ skull fracture, subdural hemorrhage or hematoma, bone fracture, dislocation/sprains, internal injuries, poisoning, burns/scalds, severe cuts/lacerations/bruises/welts, or any combination thereof " (Denver Research Institute, 1981, pp. 3-32) would be assigned to this category. Less serious injuries inflicted on the child which do not pose a substantial risk to his/her well being are classified as minor physical injuries. Only about one of every seven (14.7 percent, 3,108 of 21,086) of the reports of physical abuse included in this study were classified as 'major.' In the face of rising rates of reported child maltreatment, a reduction in the severity of investigated cases is presumed to indicate an increase in public awareness and reporting rather than in the actual prevalence of abuse and neglect. Michigan and South Carolina did not differentiate between physical abuse resulting in minor vs. major injury to the child. Their physical abuse cases were 'mapped' into the unspecified maltreatment category by the American Humane Association. Therefore, just 16 states with 815 counties were used in analyses of physical abuse.

The American Humane Association definition of sexual maltreatment includes

the involvement of a child in any sexual act or situation, the purpose of which is to provide sexual gratification or financial benefit to the perpetrator; all sexual activity between an adult and a child is considered as sexual maltreatment. (Denver Research Institute, 1981, pp. 3-34)

This description is straightforward and widely agreed upon by child protection professionals. Sexual abuse may take the forms of:

1. exploitation, which involves pornography, prostitution and other types types of immoral sexual activity in which the perpetrator does not personally interact with the child
2. incest, entailing a child's sexual activity with a blood-related adult or sibling older than 10 years of age
3. molestation, which includes such actions as the stroking of the genitals of a male child or the breasts of a female

4. other sexual maltreatment connoting indecent exposure of the child or sodomy or some other sexual activity with the child not appropriate to any of the previously delineated categories

Certain elements of the American Humane Association's definition of neglect are critical to this analysis because the incidence of child neglect was greater than for any other form of maltreatment. "It includes neglecting to provide the following when able to do so: nourishment, clothing, shelter, health care, education, supervision or causing failure to thrive" (Denver Research Institute, 1981, pp. 3-35). The reference to failure-to-thrive is in practice, of course, limited to non-organic failure-to-thrive, since parents cannot influence cases of known physiological origin. Therefore, only the non-organic variety has received the attention of professionals in the child protection field. The ability to provide is a judgment which requires the child protective worker to prioritize the needs of all members of the family. The worker's prioritization may or may not be consistent with that of family members. Information from the American Humane Association was used to profile families in which children were maltreated in 1980. Data reported to the American Humane Association varied by state. Reporting tended to be complete on variables that did not require child protection workers to make a subjective professional judgment or request information of members of the abusive family that they would normally regard as threatening. Therefore, objective data such as the race of the child and the relationship, if any, of the perpetrator to the child were almost always reported. By contrast, subjective judgments such as the presence or absence of family stresses were frequently omitted from investigative worker reports of findings. Identification of stress factors necessitates requesting information from abusive parents who are at times uncooperative or even obstructive to the efforts of the child protection worker. A reluctance on the part of the alleged perpetrator to reveal information concerning the status of the family with respect to receipt of public assistance is also understandable. The child protection worker is a representative of the department of social services which bestows the benefits of public assistance programs upon recipients whose eligibility it has certified. Individuals accused of mistreating children, who perceive that their offense could jeopardize continued enrollment in certain entitlement programs, have a motive for withholding this information. Also because abusive adults often refuse treatment unless it is court ordered, some may view termination of their participation in benefit programs as a means of leverage available to the social service department to coerce compliance with the provisions of their treatment plan. Thus, a special procedure was implemented in examining two important variables, abusive family stress factors and public assistance status to preclude the possibility of bias due to non-reporting.

Child protection workers in Michigan reported the public assistance status of all abusive and neglectful families. All records of child mistreatment occurring in New Mexico in 1980 contained information pertaining to family stress factors. Public assistance status and family stress factor data for these two states were compared directly with the aggregate data from all other study states to determine the possibility of bias due to underreporting.

In this study, the county serves as the unit of analysis for two fundamental reasons. First, data from available secondary sources are presented predominantly at the county level. For the Area Resource File, it is the only geopolitical unit for which information has been collected. Second and more importantly, this country's child protection system is operated through units headquartered in county offices of departments of social service. The matching of service with need must focus on the demands made upon those county departments and their capacity to respond. Failure to distribute professional personnel in accordance with geographic concentration of need for service causes inequity of caseload among workers which is likely to manifest itself in the quality of the service they provide.

Later presented results of this study indicate that analyses which differentiate by county population are the most useful in determining social correlates of child maltreatment.

2

Child Protection in the U.S.:
A System in Crisis

Child protection workers are the front-line professionals charged with primary responsibility in perhaps the most sensitive area of human service. They often labor without definitive procedural guidelines in a difficult and demanding environment. The public is outraged when injury or death occurs to children in their caseloads (Blampied, 1978; Fauri, 1978). But on the other hand, workers are accused of "gestapo tactics" by parents whose children they remove from the home (Lacayo, 1987). These parents typically claim overreaction resulting in violation of their parental rights. Child protection workers are confronted daily with the task of working with unmotivated family members who resent their efforts.

Their failure to provide the necessary resources to protect children has not diminished the public's demands of workers. Disappointing outcomes of the professional performance are often very 'visible.' There are two objectives fundamental to the field of child protection. Achievement of the first, the prevention of maltreatment, would of course render the second, treatment of the abusive/neglectful family, meaningless. In theory, this dichotomy is logical and to a large extent governs the division of labor within the field as well as funding priorities. In practice, treatment is also aimed at prevention, but it is tertiary prevention, that form which attempts to deter recidivism. Effort is directed at precluding further mistreatment. In some cases the task entails disruption of patterns of abusive parental behavior which have been sustained for years. When these patterns prove to be impervious to therapy, termination of parental rights becomes a defensible option. If the worker fears that the child might be harmed before all reasonable treatment options for the parents have been exhausted, the child may be temporarily removed from the home to ensure his/her immediate safety.

The term 'treatment' is not a genuine misnomer for the activities of child protection personnel seeking to change abusive parental attitudes and behaviors. The worker might focus on the perpetrator's substance abuse, or try to elevate his self-esteem, or modify basic family interactions in much the same way as a therapist working with a client or patient with any one of many mental health problems which bear no apparent relationship to child abuse.

Mental health treatment frequently has abstract goals for which there is no single related tangible outcome. The therapist sometimes seeks to change the general orientation of the patient toward life. Actual behavioral change is not always an objective. A patient's feeling better about himself may be viewed as treatment success. The child protection worker can be justifiably encouraged by therapeutic progress which presumably will lead to the intended behavioral change. But the ultimate goal of the worker is the well-being of the victimized child. It is not a negotiable matter in which either the client or therapist has prerogative.

Accountability rests almost exclusively on the worker's success in attaining such outcomes as the redirection of parental hostility away from the child, prohibiting the parent from making sexual advances toward the child, or stimulating the parent to attend to the physical and emotional needs of the child. Anything less will not suffice in the eyes of most members of the general public, many of whom take great pleasure in scrutinizing, but not subsidizing, the efforts of child protection personnel. Workers do not have broad, ambiguous performance criteria. Public expectation of them is clear. Failure to meet that expectation seldom escapes public notice.

A system staffed by dedicated, but seriously overworked personnel has been entrusted with the protection of children in this country (Antler, 1982; Daley, 1979; Harrison, 1980; Martin & Klaus, 1979). The National Center on Child Abuse and Neglect has called for renewed emphasis on comprehensive approaches to prevention since the child protective services system simply does not have the capacity to effectively handle the growing number of reports of child abuse and neglect (DHHS, 1988). Polier (1979) described the frustration CPS workers experience from their attempts to overcome the formidable barriers which prevent them from delivering needed services and later having to witness the result of not meeting the needs of children and their abusive parents. Professionals must bear responsibility for the consequences of what they fail to do with perpetrators and victims of child maltreatment just as they must for what they do with these individuals (Polier, 1979).

Increasingly, child mistreatment cases have found their way into state courts. Accused perpetrators, when informed of their inclusion in child abuse and neglect registries maintained by departments of social service, have appealed those decisions and, in cases involving removal of their children from the home or termination of parental rights, have entered into litigation against the state. Child protection workers have been cross-examined during their court testimony by counsel for alleged perpetrators. Their inability to make convincing, cogent arguments for their decisions to disrupt families even temporarily, no matter how abnormal, has been a source of humiliation for workers. They are required to make critical determinations which are then challenged in a manner which brings little credit to their efforts or professional identity.

Workers hurriedly perform critical professional tasks in a fashion analogous to the activities of emergency room personnel in the general hospital of a large metropolitan area. There, demand for care dwarfs the capacity to provide it. A normal method of triage might be to simply permit a diarrheic patient to remain in the waiting room till sufficiently rehydrated to return home. Faced with a dearth of resources, child protection workers adopt a similar mindset. They carefully and quickly screen the many cases in their caseloads to determine those which pose the greatest threat of bodily harm or permanent consequences to child victims. Regrettably, other serious situations may attract only modest professional efforts aimed at remediation. In a milieu in which service cannot possibly be made commensurate with need, imprecision is commonplace. Workers admit to lacking confidence in the criteria they use for professional decision making (Fryer et al., 1988) and misjudgment has been chronicled time after time.

Because of job pressure and low professional esteem, worker burnout and attrition have been a long-standing concern within the child protection field (Antler, 1982; Armstrong, 1979; Daley, 1979; Harrison, 1980; Jayaratne, Chess, & Kunkel, 1986; Kahn, 1978; Martin & Klaus, 1979; Maslach, 1978). Yet some of this concern has shifted from the departure of personnel from the profession to the performance of those who remain (Fryer, Miyoshi, & Thomas, 1989). Research now suggests that the worker's hurried relationship with abusive parents is combative (Fryer, Poland, Bross & Krugman, 1988) and that there is a tendency to fail to substantiate the occurrence of abuse or neglect in spite of convincing evidence in order to prevent case assignment to a treatment worker's caseload which is already excessive (American Humane Association, 1984; DHHS, 1988). While there is no doubt that the supply of workers is not sufficient to meet existing child protection needs, it now appears that maximum use of available personnel is not being made. Geographic maldistribution may also hinder effectiveness of the system. The results of a recently conducted national survey reveal that the burden of attending to the needs of abused and/or neglected children is not equitably distributed throughout the United States (Fryer et al., 1988). Worker caseloads vary remarkably geographically. While child protection personnel in some agencies were genuinely overwhelmed by the number of reports of maltreatment, workers serving elsewhere were not. The allocation of personnel resources has not been sensitive to the need for service.

The popularity of needs assessment research has grown through the years due to increasing public acceptance of the view that the allocation of resources in response to human need should be objectively founded on the results of rigorous scientific methods. Thus, a strong statistical orientation has characterized some attempts to ascertain the etiology of social problems and the size and location of needy populations. The primary purpose of needs assessment activities in the child protection field should be to anticipate the occurrence of child maltreatment "in order to achieve prevention or prompt intervention" (Galdston, 1979, p. 340).

To date, these activities have not been impressive. But the act of assessing need implies an intention to change social arrangements in a manner which alleviates the plight of persons somehow disadvantaged (Perlman & Gurin, 1972). Society has not proven itself willing to provide the resources necessary to preclude the recurrence of past failures of the U.S. Child Protection System.

3

Rival Theories and Previous Research

There is serious professional disagreement regarding the causes of child maltreatment and the theory most useful in designing interventions to prevent abuse and neglect and treat its victims. Even among the proponents of an environmental explanation of the problem, there is discord concerning which social phenomena are related to maltreatment and their relative influences. In their haste to stem growth in the prevalence of the problem and the associated suffering among victimized youth, the clinical and scientific communities have actively pursued solutions through research. It has ranged in type from clinical observation to carefully conducted case control studies.

This chapter presents the results of previous research. It reviews studies which facilitated the emergence of ecological theory, and those that underlie the chief competing and antithetical theory. Research will then be presented which suggests environmental correlates of child maltreatment, the ecological variables used in this study.

Psychodynamic vs. Sociological Theory

Initial theory concerning the etiology of child abuse and neglect emphasized almost exclusively psychological determinants. The first models designed to predict abuse and estimate incidence, therefore, focused on the individual traits of parental perpetrators. Kempe (1969) contended that the psychodynamics of child maltreatment have nothing to do with income, education, or any other variables embraced by the sociologist. All adults are said to have the potential to abuse their children (Cameron, 1970). This position has been articulated by some of the most prominent figures in the field of child welfare today:

Child abuse is not a black problem, a brown problem, or a white problem. Child abusers are found in the ranks of the unemployed, the blue-collar worker, the white-collar worker and the professional. They are Protestant, Catholic, Jewish, Baptist and atheist. (Fraser, 1976, p. 13)

Child abuse and child neglect afflict all communities regardless of race, religion or economic status. (Besharov & Besharov, 1977, p. 6)

The problem of child abuse is not limited to any particular economic, social, or intellectual level, race or religion. (Fontana, 1977 p. 505)

Child abuse and neglect occur among families from all socioeconomic levels, religious groups, races and nationalities. (Steele, 1975, p. 3)

According to many proponents of this pure psychological perspective, abusive parents have themselves been subjected to harsh child rearing practices during their childhoods. Actually, Chesser in 1952 had traced parental abuse of their children to the parents' serious psychological disorders stemming from their own abuse during childhood. Thus, treatment professionals have historically focused on the life histories of abusive parents, in addition to their psychological functioning at the beginning of therapy. An intergenerational cycle of insensitivity to children is formed quite aside from any external social influence, leading to the view that clinical intervention is the sole plausible means of remediation. Treatment protocols seldom take into account environmental conditions which shape the broad context in which abuse occurs.

Therapy addresses directly the variety of psychological problems believed characteristic of neglectful and/or abusive parents (Delsordo, 1963). Their personal shortcomings include simple immaturity and feelings of being inconvenienced by their children (Resnick, 1969; Smith, 1975) whom they blame for their own problems and those of the family. Attitudes of overpowering dependence ultimately drive some of these parents to compete with their children for the affection of the other spouse (Merrill, 1962). They tend to be disappointed with their children and dissatisfied in the role of primary caretaker (Galdston, 1965; Steele & Pollock, 1965). Their inflexible, dispassionate and unforgiving child-rearing practices are seen to derive from those to which they were subjected as children.

The phenomenon of role reversal, connoting the abusive parent's expectation that the child should meet the parent's emotional needs, has been used to describe the underlying etiology of inter-generational child maltreatment (Blumberg, 1974; Green, 1976; Helfer, 1973). Because parents are resentful of the child's inability to fulfill their needs in the way the parent would normally be expected to meet the needs of the child, they resort to abuse.

A summarization of both the psychoanalytic and behaviorist interpretations of the intergenerational cycle of abuse put forth by clinicians and researchers has been offered by Kelly (1983):

> investigators have interpreted the relationship between a parent's history of childhood abuse and the parent's current abusive behavior toward his or her own child in various ways, including psychoanalyticall (e.g., a failure to identify with a mothering role and an anger at one's own parents directed instead toward one's child) and behaviorally (e.g., imitatively learning the violent child-management practices exhibited by one's own parents). (p. 19)

Psychodynamic theory enjoyed uncontested popularity during the 1960's immediately following recognition of child abuse as a serious problem of our society. Yet, evidence of prevention and treatment success is conspicuous by its absence. Analyses that have been undertaken in an effort to evaluate the efficacy of treatment of abusive families generally indicate that most often not much progress is made toward the achievement of therapeutic objectives (Sudia, 1981). The services provided have often not even prevented revictimization of the child (Cohn, 1979). The strong objection of care-providing professions such as psychiatry, social work, and psychology to making law enforcement agencies aware of possible cases of abuse reflects their presumption that parents who maltreat their children are sick and require treatment for their care (Gil, 1970). Unfortunately, their illnesses are apparently not amenable to common therapeutic intervention.

Researchers and clinicians who subscribe to the psychodynamic perspective usually psychologically profile adult perpetrators of child maltreatment. They have characterized abusive parents by their personal attributes and past experiences: individual deficits are said to account for deviant destructive acts. But research findings have not been consistent (Gelles, 1973) and as the disappointing outcomes of treatment plainly indicate, psychodynamic theory has not been an especially effective guide for widespread clinical application.

Pelton (1981) has argued that the psychodynamic model has endured in the face of apparent practical discreditation, because:

> the professional helping establishment has overly psychologized the problems of child abuse and neglect. The psychodynamic orientation in the context of a medical model of disease, treatment, and cure, has unquestionably become the dominant viewpoint within the field. Yet the facts increasingly point to the major role that social and economic factors play in child maltreatment, and to the need for services that address the situational context of abuse and neglect than for

psychotherapeutic treatment of the parents themselves. Because many helping professionals, and the general public, have become so enamored of psychological analyses and solutions of social problems, the socioeconomic viewpoint of child maltreatment has received far less exposure, and in fact has been relatively ignored. (p. 11)

Antler (1981) also took issue with imposing a medical perspective onto what should be viewed as a social concern. This has resulted in radical alteration of the broader approach which had evolved in the fifty year period preceding Dr. Kempe's introduction of the 'battered child syndrome.' The status and credibility of the medical profession was, however, clearly an asset in the promotion of child abuse as an issue of the utmost importance in this country.

Kenniston (1979) states that the individual orientation of Americans will not be easily set aside:

Americans have been profoundly influenced by a tradition of individualism that makes it hard for us to perceive the larger causes of social ills. Since our very founding we have emphasized the freedom of the individual, the opportunities of the individual, and the responsibilities of the individual. And, historically, we have also invariably tended to credit primarily the individual for his or her place on the social ladder. And this, of course, has given rise to our long custom of blaming individually those of us who have wound up suffering financial or social or moral perplexities. Out of that perception has come the long--and largely unsuccessful-- history of our efforts to cure our social ailments by reforming and uplifting those individuals whom we have viewed as short on character or morality. (p. 284)

If the psychodynamic orientation is to be displaced, another must be made ready and earn the favor of scholars, professionals, and policy makers. Sociological theory has become firmly entrenched as the antithesis to the psychodynamic approach, but has not yet gained wide public or professional acceptance. Garbarino and Stocking (1980) have written capably of the need to expand our perception of the problem of child abuse to include the social context in which maltreatment occurs:

In our society, we typically see child abuse and neglect--as we do all problems--as the result of an individual deficiency. We concentrate on parents who are mentally ill or have unrealistic expectations about what children can and should not do. We focus on the pathological upbringing that makes a person unsuited for the demanding task of parenthood, or we look to the mismatch between parents' needs and children's needs. As a result of this orientation, we typically seek cures that emphasize individual rehabilitation and therapy. Without dismissing the importance of this individualistic perspective, and with full recognition that each case of child abuse and neglect has its own special origins, we would like to suggest that abuse and neglect are not only problems of individual abusers and their victims but are also problems of the social contexts in which these individuals live. (pp. 1-2)

Failure to appreciate the importance of social circumstance to human behavior has been represented as a significant shortcoming of many psychologists Ross, 1977). The ecological approach developed by Bronfenbrenner (1977) constitutes a serious theoretical effort toward remediation. This approach recognizes the influence society and social units such as communities have on human behavior. Environment is seen as a dictate of family life. Indirect, 'second-order' effects of their surroundings mediate parent-child interaction. Concern must be placed not on "who cares for children, but on who cares for those who care for those who care for children" (Bronfenbrenner, 1978, p. 777). This perspective implies the necessity for a shift of emphasis in prevention programming from the pathology of individuals to that pathology generally associated with certain environments (Garbarino & Stocking, 1980). It has been labeled the 'ecological' perspective.

Bronfenbrenner (1979, p. 231) recommended that scholars who maintain the ecological perspective focus on "interaction between the developing organism and the enduring environments or contexts in which it lives out its life." Familiar trends toward single-parent families and unwed mothers have constituted subject matter for modern ecologists. They view child abuse largely as a consequence of overwhelming changes in the American family.

The present situation has been graphically portrayed (Report to the President, White House Conference on Children):

In today's world parents find themselves at the mercy of a society which imposes pressures and priorities that allow neither time nor place for meaningful activities and relations between children and adults, which downgrade the role of parents and the functions of parenthood, and which prevent the parent from doing things he wants to do as a guide, friend, and companion to his children . . . The frustrations are greatest for the family of poverty where the capacity for human response is crippled by hunger cold, filth, sickness, and despair. For families who can get along, the rats are gone, but the rat-race remains. The demands of a job, or often two jobs, that claim mealtimes, evenings, and weekends as well as days; the trips and moves necessary to get ahead or simply hold one's own; the ever increasing time spent in commuting, parties, evenings out, social and community obligations--all the things one has to do to meet so-called primary responsibilities--produce a situation in which a child often spends more time with a passive babysitter than a participating parent. (p. 240)

The American family has surrendered its identity as a 'nurturing oasis' (Kenniston, 1979). Freud (1950) warned that a parent's instinct to nurture coexisted with an impulse to injure the young. From the nurturant oasis, the family has been transformed into both an agent and arena for violence (Gil, 1979).

Garbarino and Sherman (1980), who examined the attributes of geographic units in much the same manner as others have studied the family, concluded that community characteristics were meaningful to understanding patterns of child abuse and neglect. They identified neighborhoods as high or low risk units on the basis of their characteristics, just as parents are sometimes seen as 'at risk' to abuse their children. The authors advocated the use of data on social conditions to make risk designations. Neighborhoods differ, according to Warren (1980), in the intensity with which residents relate to their immediate surroundings and the community at large. Each neighborhood affords its inhabitants a certain capacity to solve their personal and family problems, through resources which Warren (1980) terms 'problem-solving pathways.' These should be fully understood by child protection professionals involved in cases of abuse occurring there.

Sociologists have made comparisons between abusive parents on the one hand and adults in the general population on the other, on socioeconomic demographics such as income, occupational status, and level of education. Empirical studies have yielded information more useful to prevention efforts than the anecdotal data produced by earlier clinical observation of very small samples. Other sociological researchers have surveyed just families in which child abuse was known to have taken place. Most have found that parents from lower social strata are overrepresented among their samples (Giovannoni & Billingsley, 1970; Pelton, 1978).

Elmer (1981), on the basis of the findings of a follow-up study of traumatized children, has argued that the inclusion of socioeconomic factors can bring much needed balance to the investigation of the causes of child maltreatment:

The malignant effects of abuse and neglect are by no means questioned; what is questioned is the singular, intense focus on abuse without regard for the matrix in which it flourishes. Of course there are other reasons besides poverty for the playing out of abusive impulses, but poverty has been proved to be the fertile soil that incubates and nourishes a variety of social problems that might wither away in a more comfortable social class. (pp. 211-212)

This hopeless milieu in which the propensity to mistreat is strong has been depicted by Coles (1979):

Everywhere things go wrong: the lights don't work, the stairs are treacherous; rats constantly appear, and they are not timid, uniformed men patrol the streets, certain that trouble will appear; teachers work in schools they are ashamed to call their own, at work they judge hopeless, under a bureaucratic system that stifles them, that is, if they are still alive; jobs are few, and welfare is the essence of the economy. (p. 294)

Garbarino and Stocking (1980) explained the view of most ecological theorists that income influences parent-child relations, but that secure financial status is not a guarantor against abuse. Economic means hedge or cushion against an individual's personal failings, but give no assurance that parental personal deficiencies will not lead to abusive behavior. The authors concede that there is a powerful link between economic status and social behavior, but point out that the stresses of daily life may overwhelm the wealthy while the most impoverished setting may be the site for exemplary child-rearing by strong parents dedicated to the well-being of their children.

Kelly (1983) also cautioned against unwarranted inference concerning the relationship of socioeconomic status to child abuse:

Many studies examining SES factors in relation to child abuse find evidence that reported child maltreatment is correlated with social and economic stress. While most investigators are careful to avoid inferring a direct causal relationship between poverty and child abuse, the life stressors of families living with only marginal social and economic supports can be conducive to the development of frustration and violence, including child maltreatment. This certainly does not mean that child abuse is limited to families subjected to socioeconomic stress, nor that most families under even severe SES stress abuse their children. It only indicates that the reported frequency of child maltreatment appears to be associated with indices of social and economic disadvantage. (p. 18)

Thus, studies which find common attributes among abusive families have been criticized by Calam and Franchi (1987) as permitting only limited conclusions to be drawn from their results. They point out that determination of specific families in which abuse will ultimately occur is the single worthy goal of research in the field. Admittedly, predictive certainty in this regard is unattainable. But identification of characteristics of families in which child maltreatment is most common can meaningfully inform prevention efforts.

Studies of the relationship of socioeconomic disadvantage to rates of child mistreatment, which has relied principally on large probability samples in gathering demographic data on families, have produced a viable response to the earlier posed question concerning persistence of the psychodynamic orientation. Pelton (1981) perceived the popularity of psychodynamic theory to be its provision to shift blame from the conditions of poverty to the individual who suffers from those conditions:

> Both evidence and reason lead to the unmistakable conclusion that, contrary to the myth of classlessness, child abuse and neglect are strongly related to poverty, in terms of prevalence and of severity of consequences. This is not to say that abuse and neglect do not occur among other socioeconomic classes, or that, when they do occur, they never have severe consequences. However, widespread reports suggesting that abuse and neglect are classless phenomena are unfounded and misleading. The myth of classlessness persists not on the basis of evidence or logic, but because it serves certain professional and political interests. These interests do not further the task of dealing with the real problems underlying abuse and neglect; adherence to the myth diverts attention from the nature of the problems and diverts resources from their solution. (pp. 36-37)

Similarly, Antler (1981) noted that medicalization of child maltreatment has distracted human service professionals and the public from the critical role that social factors occupy in the etiology of abuse and has rendered the needs of the family a secondary concern. Kenniston (1979) asserts that there are social forces that no individual can withstand, and that parents and children who suffer from these influences cannot be blamed for the crippling situations in which they find themselves.

The cost of purging child abuse from our society has been represented as unacceptable to some (Gil, 1979):

> If one's priority is to prevent all child abuse, one must be ready to part with its many causes, even when one is attached to some of them, such as the apparent blessings, advantages, and privileges of inequality. If, on the other hand, one is reluctant to give up all aspects of the causal context of child abuse, one must be content to continue living with this social problem. In that latter case, one ought to stop talking about

primary prevention and face the fact that all one may be ready for is some measure of amelioration. (p. 17)

The perpetrator is a 'scapegoat' for a society that has come to realize that eradication of child maltreatment is only possible at considerable cost to its more affluent members. Current therapeutic interventions do not approach the expense of mounting a serious attack on the social deprivation associated with poverty. The purpose of a comprehensive, but costly and obtrusive, ecological assault on child mistreatment would be to improve systematically the environment in which the members of families interact.

Identification of the specific environmental correlates of abuse and neglect are prerequisite to such an 'ecological assault' on the problem. Previous research indicates the importance of a number of social phenomena to the etiology of child maltreatment.

Adolescent Pregnancy and Illegitimate Birth

Illegitimate pregnancies and unwanted births to adolescent women have been found to be associated with child mistreatment (Baldwin, 1977; Bennett & Pethybridge, 1979; Bolton, 1981; Creighton, 1979; Gagan, Cupoli, & Watkins, 1984; Gelles, 1985; Jameson & Schellenbach, 1977; Kaplun & Reich, 1976; McCarthy, 1981; O'Donnell et al., 1982; Okeahialam, 1984; Schene, 1984; Smith, 1975; Smith, Hanson, & Noble, 1974; Trube-Becker, 1977; Usdan, 1978; Wethers, 1978). These mothers are viewed as children who themselves have children. They are particularly ill-prepared for the responsibilities of motherhood, and they themselves have often suffered mistreatment at the hands of their parents (Jameson & Schellenbach, 1977).

Schene (1984) examined census data for the general population of the United States along with information from more than 400,000 cases of reported child abuse and neglect. Analysis of these data indicated that both children and parents were young in cases of parental neglect. Households were female-headed since the mother was frequently unmarried. Friends and neighbors reported parental neglect, but professionals more often reported abusive behavior to departments of social service.

In a broad overview of violence in the American family, Gelles (1985) reviewed the findings of a probability sample of 2,143 U.S. families drawn in 1976. The researcher projected from the results of this sample that 1.6 million children, or 3.6 percent of all those between the ages of 3 and 17, were abused. Abuse was defined in the survey as punching, kicking, biting, beating, hitting with an object, and threatening with a knife or gun. Perpetrating parents were youthful and tended to hold either agnostic or atheistic religious beliefs.

Women less than 15 years old were found particularly abusive in a study of correlates of maltreatment conducted by O'Donnell et al. (1982) and by Bolton (1981). Adolescents also tend to deliver infants who fail to thrive (Gagan, Cupoli, & Watkins, 1984). Unfortunately, these immature mothers also lack a developed social network to which they can turn in times of crisis. Jameson and Schellenbach (1977) found that female perpetrators were much younger than men who mistreat children. Many women perpetrators had records of having been abused in their own youth. Bolton (1981) assessed 63 mothers between 13 and 19 years of age in the hospital on the first day after having given birth. Follow-up, in-home interviews were also administered for these adolescent mothers, 76.7 percent of whom were not married. About half received public assistance and many were ignorant of sound child-rearing practices and the proper parental relationship with the child. Bolton (1981) concluded that the needs of these young women were varied and numerous, and that when these needs remained unmet, adolescent mothers were inclined to react violently toward their children.

This same relationship has been observed in countries other than the United States. In 54 cases of child death due to parental neglect in West Germany, mothers of the deceased children were regarded as simply too young and immature to perform their parental responsibilities (Trube-Becker, 1977). Examination of 905 child abuse cases reported during 1976 revealed that early parenthood was a frequent characteristic of abusive parents in England (Creighton, 1979). Young parents often inflicted severe child abuse in a mixed urban and rural community in that country (Baldwin, 1977). Parental youth was also a characteristic of perpetrators of especially brutal cases of mistreatment in which illegitimate preschoolers were the usual victims of child homicides in New York City from 1968 through 1969 (Kaplun & Reich, 1976).

Also in England, in a two-year study performed at the University of Birmingham, parents who had abused 134 children younger than five years old were compared with a matched group of non-abusive parents whose children had been admitted to the hospital for an emergency (Smith, 1975; Smith, Hanson & Noble, 1974). Abusive parents were four years younger than the British average at the time of first birth. The mean age of children who had been maltreated was just 1.5 years.

The highest rate of child abuse in Georgia during a four-year period was among mothers with an early childbearing age (McCarthy, 1981). Over half had become pregnant as adolescents out of wedlock. Increased childbearing among adolescents has been cited as one of the social phenomena responsible for drastic increases in child maltreatment in American families (Usdan, 1978). Wethers (1978) also noted this same societal factor as a contributor to abuse.

Divorce and Marital Discord

Changes in the structure of the American family have been suggested as an influence on the increasing tendency toward violence directed against children and spouses by other family members. Divorce and the marital discord leading to marital dissolution are important components of that scenario (Ayoub & Pfeifer, 1979; Finkelhor, 1982; Holman & Kanwar, 1975; Mayer & Black, 1977; Mehta et al., 1979; Philips, 1983; Smith, Hanson, & Noble, 1974; Solnit, 1978; Wight, 1969).

The children of parents who divorce suffer the economic effects usually inherent in separations of spouses who are required to make substantial adaptations to their vastly changed family situation (Philips, 1983). The stress which derives from economic and social change following marital disruption precipitates child maltreatment (Baker, 1982). An increasing rate of divorce in this country and abroad is thought to have especially affected the incidence of sexual abuse (Finkelhor, 1982).

A multidisciplinary child abuse team examined 26 children who had been injured in a two-year period (Ayoub & Pfeifer, 1979). Marital conflicts and family violence were more prevalent among the families whose injuries had not been accidental. The child sometimes serves as a magnet for parental attacks in violent, unhappy families. Thus, the rising divorce rate that symbolizes the stressful era in which the nuclear family now finds itself is understandably linked to an increased incidence of child maltreatment (Solnit, 1978).

Seventy-seven infants were surveyed longitudinally for a full year to determine the relationship between injuries they had incurred and their home environment (Wight, 1969). Many of the children came from broken homes marked by very stressful environments. Holman and Kanwar (1975) also found that problems among spouses were common features of a poor environment which leads to child maltreatment. Absence of the child's father and marital disharmony were precursors to physical abuse of children from 214 abusive families who took part in a two-year study (Smith, Hanson & Noble, 1974).

The Single-Parent Family

Another structural variable is the spousal configuration of the family, which in fact can be the result of divorce. Single parent families (Billingsley, 1980; Caplan et al., 1984; Garbarino, 1981; Meier, 1985; Scherzer & Lala, 1980; Solnit, 1978; Usdan, 1978), particularly female-headed families, are overrepresented among abusive families (Chunn, 1980; Garbarino, 1976; Schene, 1984; Sutherland, 1976; Smith, Hanson & Noble, 1974). The lone parent present must carry the huge burden of caring for the children and earning the wages sufficient to meet the needs of the family members. Stresses associated with this dual role, and sometimes the scars of a marriage gone sour, take their toll over time, disposing the parent to abusive behavior. Actual fatigue on the part of single parents has been reported as a precipitating factor in abuse (Meier, 1985).

Records for 422 cases of child maltreatment that occurred during a five-year period in Toronto were reviewed by Caplan et al. (1984). A large proportion of single-parent families existed among the sample. Aside from the fact that the parents had no spouse with whom to interact, these individuals were otherwise socially isolated as well.

In 1978, 73 cases were analyzed at the Baltimore City Hospital. Half involved children from single-parent families (Scherzer & Lala, 1980). Single-parent families are thought to be most heavily concentrated in poor neighborhoods and constitute a severe drain on the few support resources that are located there (Garbarino, 1981).

Billingsley (1980) discovered through a two-state survey of 1,087 households in 10 cities that single-parent households negatively influenced the quality of child care in the midwestern region surveyed. Usdan (1978) and Solnit (1978) argued that the growing number of children being cared for outside the home is due to the absolute and proportional increase of women in the labor force.

Chunn (1980) collected data in an effort to identify differences between abusive vs. non-abusive black mothers. Of the 224 women who took part in this study, 103 were known to have abused their children. Even though abusing mothers had a larger number of children to care for, they usually did not have the benefit of a male spouse to share those duties.

Female-headed households frequently have been the setting for child neglect (Schene, 1984; Sutherland, 1976). Moreover, single-parent females have also been found to abuse their young children more often than in two-parent families. These women often not only attempt to raise their children without the father of the children, but also without any other kin support (Smith, Hanson, & Noble, 1974).

Economic Status

The single most important area of possible correlates of child maltreatment exhaustively investigated by social scientists has been socioeconomic forces. Economic problems rooted in income insufficiency have drawn special attention (Antler, 1978; Arnold, 1982; Baker, 1982; Baldwin, 1977; Bennett & Pethybridge, 1979; Billingsley, 1980; Ceresnie and Starr, 1977; Chunn, 1980; Creighton, 1979; Dibble, 1982; Dibble and Straus, 1980;

Downing, 1980; Gagan, Cupoli & Watkins, 1984; Garbarino, 1981; Garbarino, Sherman, & Crouter, 1979; Garbarino, 1976; Gelles, 1985; Gil, 1969, 1985; Kent et al., 1983; Krugman, 1984; Loening, 1981; Lowrey, 1978; Mehta et al., 1979; Morse et al., 1979; National Indian Child Abuse and Neglect Resource Center, 1980; Newberger & Newberger, 1980; Okeahialam, 1984; Parton, 1980; Pelton, 1978; Ritchie & Ritchie, 1981; Sattin & Miller, 1971; Schene, 1984; Schmidt, 1977; Silver, 1968; Spearly & Lauderdale, 1983; Steinberg, Catalano, & Dooley, 1981; Steinmetz, 1980; Straus, 1978; Sutherland, 1976; Weaver, 1976; Wight, 1969). Child abuse is represented as the product of frustrations that stem from economic deprivation. Child maltreatment is a manifestation of the hardship imposed by economic obstacles to meeting family member needs.

Low income groups provide a disproportionately large percentage of the abusive families whose cases are handled by multidisciplinary child protection teams (Krugman, 1984). Insufficient family income has been associated with social stress, based on the results of a survey of a huge representative sample of U.S. families, and that stress in turn produced the physical abuse of children (Gelles, 1985).

A case control study of 20 abusive families who visited hospital emergency rooms and 20 nonabusive families was conducted by Ceresnie and Starr (1977). Income and other economic factors determined assignment to two comparison groups. These factors were correlates of stress and poor mother-child interaction. Poor impulse control among abusive parents has been attributed to economic stress to which they are subjected (Baker, 1982). Changes in the economy have exacerbated socioeconomic structural inequality and hastened the increase in observed parental violence toward their children (Parton, 1985).

In certain underdeveloped third world countries children have been introduced prematurely to the pressures of the labor force, and have been otherwise exploited in an effort to enhance family income and economic standing (Okeahialam, 1984). Arnold (1982) employed displacement theory to explain child maltreatment in the West Indies. The difficulties of economically disadvantaged adults are transformed into stress which is 'displaced' by harsh treatment of their children. Child abuse in Polynesia was studied through review of the findings of ethnographic research (Ritchie & Ritchie, 1981). Low socioeconomic status and European influences on child-rearing were found to account for observed patterns of abuse. The spread of poverty among the Zulu people, also attributable to Westernization and industrialization of overcrowded cities, corresponded to hospital reports of severe child maltreatment (Loening, 1981).

Examination of census and child abuse registry data for 246 counties in the state of Texas revealed that general economic status of that geopolitical unit can influence rates of child maltreatment (Spearly & Lauderdale, 1983).

The lower the percentage of all families with incomes exceeding $15,000 per year, the greater the reported incidence of child abuse and neglect. The amount of public assistance provided to the needy was also a factor. Greater financial assistance to the poor was found to curtail the prevalence of violence directed toward children.

Direct comparisons were made between demographic characteristics of persons involved in child abuse cases in the state of Oklahoma vs. other states (Downing, 1980). This analysis included identification of differences in rates of maltreatment and type. Regions with sizable populations of low income people had higher incidence rates of reported child mistreatment than did other areas. Garbarino (1981) observed this phenomenon at the neighborhood level. Poor neighborhoods tended to be characterized by transiency, single-parent families, and other factors that contribute to child abuse and neglect. These areas are inhabited by persons who are increasingly vulnerable economically, as the job market for unskilled workers shrinks in conjunction with technological advance in society (Billingsley, 1980). Sattin and Miller 1971) found from their study of rates of child abuse among military households in El Paso, Texas, that run-down neighborhoods inhabited by low-income families were the setting in which maltreatment was most prevalent.

Undesirable changes in the economy of an area have also been shown to affect the incidence of child abuse and neglect (Steinberg, Catalano, & Dooley, 1981). A longitudinal study of two distinct metropolitan counties in the Los Angeles area was conducted over a 30-month period. A causal chain involving both income/unemployment and stress was established. Job loss, or even the anticipation of unemployment created a stressful condition which led to increased child abuse.

Garbarino, Sherman and Crouter (1979) employed census tracts as their unit of analysis in examining correlates of child mistreatment in a single Nebraska county. Reports of abuse and neglect were obtained from state and local child protection agencies. Economic variables accounted for 38 percent of the total variance in rates of maltreatment. The impact of economic stresses was somewhat mediated, however, by the presence and extent of family support systems. Garbarino (1976) had earlier employed U.S. Census data to consider ecological causes of child maltreatment in the counties of New York State. A similar result of 36 percent of the variance in mistreatment rates was attributable to socioeconomic stresses not mitigated by systems of family support.

Patterns of child physical abuse were examined by interviewing parents in a nationally representative sample of 1,146 families with at least one child between 3 and 17 years of age (Straus, 1978). Fourteen percent of all children within that age group were found to have been physically abused during the period of a year. Comparison of abusive vs. non-abusive families suggested that economic insecurity was a major societal dynamic which contributed to child abuse.

Other researchers have directed their analyses toward extreme economic deprivation. They have specifically addressed the effects of actual impoverishment and the human degradation that accompanies poverty as correlates of child maltreatment (Antler, 1978, 1983; Baily & Baily, 1985; de Silva, 1981; Dilorenzo, 1978; Elmer, 1981; Garbarino, 1976, 1980; Gil, 1977, 1981; Kaplun & Reich, 1976; McNamee, 1982; Pelton, 1978, 1981; Quebec Ministry of Justice, 1984; Schene, 1984; Sutherland, 1976; Trube-Becker, 1977; Wolfgang, 1982). Poverty was cited by Gil (1977) as one of the alienating circumstances which contributed to the 'triggering context' for abuse. Baily and Baily (1985) noted that child abuse follows from the stress which results directly from poverty. Pelton (1981) similarly explains the strong relationship between poverty and abuse by stresses on parents created by their impoverished environment. Impoverished living conditions have also been linked to acute family stress which constitutes the impetus for parental aggression toward children (Wolfgang, 1982). Such aggression follows logically from the feelings of frustration and insecurity held by parents whose economic situation is desperate (Garbarino, 1980).

Neglect was the form of maltreatment most strongly associated with poverty in two studies conducted in Quebec (Quebec Ministry of Justice, 1984). The abandonment of children and failure to attend to even their most basic needs arose from poverty in Sri Lanka (de Silva, 1981).

In Germany, poverty was implicated in the most severe cases of neglect, those resulting in death (Trube-Becker, 1977). Fifty-four children who had died from neglect were studied. The symptomatology in these cases was hideous, e.g., emaciation, sunken eyes, aged face. These children had without exception lived in the midst of profound poverty.

In this country, the association between poverty and child death from physical abuse has been firmly established (Kaplun & Reich, 1976). Police inquiry and postmortem reports on 112 child murders were reviewed. Most of the families were known to child protection agencies and had long records of child maltreatment, which continued with the siblings of the deceased even after the homicide. The majority of these families were severely impoverished. Death usually came at the hands of a frustrated mother who killed the child in an impulsive fit of rage.

Their inability to maintain gainful employment of course contributes to, and may in some cases be the sole cause of, the impoverished conditions in which many abusive families find themselves. Some of the earlier discussed research treated the role of unemployment in the plight of poor families. Certain researchers have been explicit about the specific relationship of unemployment to the mistreatment of children (Antler, 1978, 1983; Arnold,

1982; Ayoub & Pfeifer, 1979; Billingsley, 1980; Chunn, 1980; Creighton, 1979; Dibble & Straus, 1980; Fitch & Papantonio, 1983; Jameson & Schellenbach, 1977; Krugman, 1984; Madge, 1983; Mayer & Black, 1977; McNamee, 1982; Meier, 1985; Morse et al., 1977; Newberger & Newberger, 1980; Quebec Ministry of Justice, 1984; Schene, 1984; Scherzer and Lala, 1980; Steinberg, Catalano, & Dooley, 1981; Trube-Becker, 1977; White & Cornely, 1981; Wolfgang, 1982).

Krugman (1984) reviewed cases referred to the University of Colorado child protection team at University Hospital in Denver during a twenty-year period. About half of the families in which physical abuse occurred did not have an employed spouse. Jameson and Schellenbach (1977) investigated the characteristics and family histories of 36 female and 46 male child abuse perpetrators. Unemployment was much more predictive of perpetration by males than by females.

The rate of unemployment among the families whose cases were reviewed by Krugman (1984) was very similar to that found for 73 families in the city of Baltimore in 1978 in which sexual abuse had taken place (Scherzer & Lala, 1980). Unemployment was strongly related to the severity, as well as to the frequency, of abuse in the cases analyzed by Krugman (1984). Other findings of severe brutality have been linked with the unemployment of adults in the family. Certain children who suffered from non-accidental burns and either died or incurred permanent physical handicaps had unemployed parents (Ayoub & Pfeifer, 1979). All had records of previous injuries.

Madge (1983) cautioned from a review of literature pertaining to paternal unemployment that its consequences were dependent upon social context at the time. The meaning and implications of joblessness during the depression were not the same as at the present time. Yet, the author acknowledged the wealth of survey results which attest to the contribution of unemployment to child abuse. In countries in which government benefits are not provided to mitigate the effects of unemployment, its consequences are especially harsh (Arnold, 1982). But families characterized by unemployment in the United States do usually qualify for a myriad of health and social services subsidized by public funds. Several researchers have commented on the overrepresentation of public assistance recipients among perpetrators of child maltreatment (Kaplun & Reich, 1976; Schene, 1984; Scherzer & Lala, 1980; Sokol, 1976; White & Cornely, 1981). A random sample of adult females from seven New England communities targeted those with abusive potential. These women were often receiving unemployment insurance benefits, welfare, or some other form of governmental aid. Three-fourths of the families studied by Scherzer and Lala (1980), in which children had been sexually abused, were recipients of public assistance.

Education

Education has also been portrayed as an important correlate of child maltreatment (Baldwin, 1977; Bennett & Pethybridge, 1979; Chunn, 1980; Creighton, 1979; de Silva, 1981; Dilorenzo, 1978; Downing, 1980; Fergusson, Fleming, & O'Neill, 1972; Gagan, Cupoli & Watkins, 1984; Garbarino, 1976; Gil, 1969; Jameson & Schellenbach, 1977; Kent ct al., 1983; Lowrey, 1978; Maurer, 1979; Parton, 1980; Ritchie & Ritchie, 1981; Schmidt, 1977; Steinmetz, 1980; Weaver, 1976; Wight, 1969). Most findings have indicated that perpetrators of abuse and neglect have attained a lower level of education than that which typifies the general population. This finding has been consistent irrespective of the measure of education level: average number of years of formal education, percent having completed high school, percent having graduated from college, etc.

Kent et al. (1983) conducted an empirical study of 99 court-adjudicated families in which children had suffered non-accidental trauma. One of four etiologies of child abuse derived involved either fathers or step-fathers who were poorly educated. This pattern has been traced to attitudes toward corporal punishment which conform to lines of social disparity in society (Maurer, 1979). Physical punishment of children is viewed as an acceptable child-rearing practice by undereducated parents, whereas well-educated adults exhibit disdain toward the use of physical force in parenting. Under education has been found to characterize both male and female perpetrators (Jameson & Schellenbach, 1977) in specified regions of the U.S. (Downing, 1980; Garbarino, 1976), the nation as a whole (Gil, 1969), and abroad (Bennett & Pethybridge, 1979). The preponderance of research evidence attests to the value of considering social variables in examination of the etiology of child maltreatment. Thus, the environmental variables which were related to abuse and neglect by previously discussed research were employed in the analysis described in the succeeding chapter. The 33 items extracted from public data sets for this purpose are identified and appear in Chapter IV.

4

Findings

This chapter includes brief descriptions of the study population and abusive and neglectful families, and the effect of the population of the county units on the analysis. The latter part of the chapter portrays the relationships between environmental variables and rates of child maltreatment.

The Population at Risk

The population at risk was composed of 18,942,579 persons younger than 18 years of age. They were predominantly white (15,016,999; 79.3 percent), 2,735,278 were black (14.4 percent), and 1,190,302 (6.3 percent) were members of other racial minorities. Three-fourths (14,107,307; 74.5 percent) were between the ages of 5 and 17. The remainder (4,835,272; 25.5 percent) were of preschool age. Of these children, 3,989,273 (21.1 percent) resided in counties with population less than 50,000 persons. Counties with populations between 50,000 and 100,000 were inhabited by 2,824,709 children (14.9 percent). The large majority of children in the 18 study states (12,128,597; 64.0 percent) lived in counties with population in excess of 100,000.

Although study states experienced a net loss of population through migration from 1970 to 1976, that loss of population was small in comparison to the natural increase of more than two million experienced by those states in those same six years. That trend was strongly demonstrated in 1980 when 1,049,422 live births and 584,650 deaths were recorded. A total of 12,876 children did not survive the first year of life, an infant mortality rate of 12.3 per 1,000 live births. Infancy is the period of greatest risk for child maltreatment.

Sparsely Populated Counties

During calendar year 1980, 160,060 reports of child abuse and neglect were made to certified protection agencies serving these 18 states. The 696 counties that had 1980 populations of less than 50,000 people accounted for just 18.5 percent (29,563) of all reports of child maltreatment recorded in the 18 study states. Maltreatment reports in counties with fewer than 50,000 inhabitants involved 46,470 children. This figure constitutes only 22.9 percent of the 204,404 children reportedly victimized in the 944 counties of the 18 states. One hundred fifty-three children died as a direct result of these incidents. Twenty-four (15.7 percent) of these deaths occurred in the 696 counties in which less than 50,000 persons live.

Small counties were characterized by extreme rates subject to huge variation. One of these counties recorded a rate of 73.23 reports per 1,000 children. The highest rate among counties with at least 50,000 residents was just 27.38. The standard deviation for maltreatment rates for these more sparsely settled counties considerably exceeded that for the 248 counties with larger populations (6.0 vs. 4.9). Previous research has shown that the study of correlates of child maltreatment rates in small population units can be misleading (Fryer, 1990).

In spite of these difficulties, inclusion of counties with relatively small populations is warranted for a number of important reasons.

1. A rate of 6.66 maltreatment cases per 1,000 children was observed in counties of less than 50,000 people vs. 8.8 per 1,000 children for counties with greater populations. This substantial crude difference suggests that forces associated with the maltreatment of children may be stronger or more in evidence in urban/suburban settings than in a rural environment.
2. The factors of risk for child maltreatment in small counties, as will later be shown, differ substantively from those for counties with greater populations. Socioeconomic status in less populated counties is inferior, but family structure is more stable there than in more heavily populated counties.
3. Although small population size may inhibit investigation of the correlates of of child abuse and neglect, this finding in no way minimizes the importance of child mistreatment in rural and other less populated areas. The horror of the suffering or fatality of a child at the hands of a parent or another adult is not contingent upon the nature of the community in which it occurs.

Characteristics of Abusive and
Neglectful Families

Data from the American Humane Association provide a profile of families in the 18 study states in which child maltreatment occurred in 1980. The average age of victims of child maltreatment was 7.51 years. They were about evenly divided between the sexes, with 49.1 percent being male.

Child maltreatment is enacted almost exclusively within the family unit. Of the 173,247 perpetrators of mistreatment in the 18 states, 91.8 percent (158,935) were the child's parents. Another 3.8 percent (6,570) were other family members. Mistreatment does not usually occur at a day care center, nursery school, or in the home of a babysitter. The child's home has become the scene for these acts of cruelty rather than a shelter from them.

The child's caretaker has been defined as "any natural, step, or adoptive parent or other person residing with the child who has an ongoing responsibility for his/her care and supervision" (Denver Research Institute, 1981, pp. 3-6). This does not mean that the caretaker was present when child maltreatment occurred, although the percentage of all perpetration which involved parents indicates that the caretaker usually was present. While the overwhelming majority of all families (81.5 percent; 13,977,906 of 17,158,079) in the study area included a married couple, only about half (52.5 percent; 55,107 of 104,959) of the victims in reports of abuse and neglect were children in those families in which both parents were present. Risk in the traditional two-parent family is comparatively much less than in the next most common family form. The percentage of reports for which there was only a female caretaker (41.2 percent; 43,192 of 104,959) was alarmingly high, given the modest prevalence of families headed by females (10.2 percent; 1,762,461).

Most victims of maltreatment were white Anglo children (69.4 percent; 136,446 of 196,676). Another 5.4 percent of (10,689) children who were allegedly abused or neglected were Hispanic. Therefore, almost three-fourths (74.8 percent) of all victims were Caucasian compared with 79.3 percent of the child population. Racial minorities were somewhat overrepresented among victimized children. Whereas about one-fifth (21.9 percent; 42,968) of alleged victims were black, 14.4 percent of all children residing in the study area (2,735,278) were black. Native American children comprised 1.2 percent (2,313) of maltreatment victims.

Data provided by two states were especially helpful in considering public assistance status and family stress factors. Public assistance status was obtained for all 1980 reports contained in the state child abuse and neglect registry of the state of Michigan. Michigan data encompassed 28,983 reports of child mistreatment. Of these, 16,484 (56.9 percent) involved families on public assistance. For the 59,680 reports from the 18 states that contained public assistance information, 30,116 (50.5 percent) involved families that were receiving benefits. This finding would seem to imply that there is no major bias associated with underreporting and a very high proportion of public assistance families are involved in cases of child maltreatment. However, for the 18 states, only about three of every eight reports (59,680) were annotated for public assistance status. Thus, almost one-half (48.6 percent) of all information examined for this variable was applicable to cases from Michigan, just one of the 18 states. Caution must be exercised in generalization to other geographic regions on the basis of these data.

Reporting on stress factors--health problems, economic and living difficulties, problems in family interaction and other sources of stress--was also sporadic. Most counties, 748 of 944, submitted information on this variable but usually on a small percentage of total cases. Just 46,997 report records contained data on stress factors. But the presence of the powerful effect of stress is evident among those reports. Tension which marked the interaction of family members was the category of stress factors most often observed by child protection workers (29,244 of 46,997 reports; 62.2 percent). Health problems and economic and living situation problems were recorded by workers with about equal frequency (35.2 and 37.7 percent of all cases respectively). Stress noted in many cases was not categorized (22,432; 47.7 percent).

New Mexico was the only state to annotate every 1980 record submitted to the American Humane Association with an entry describing family stress factors or the absence of stress in abusive and/or neglectful families. Workers there were required to enter this information onto the official registry record. Only 79 of the 1,424 New Mexico reports, 5.5 percent, indicated an absence of stress. A total of 2,550 stress factors were recorded, an average of 1.79 per family. The state of New Mexico with its 32 counties did not dominate reporting of stress factors as Michigan did with respect to the variable for public assistance status. Another 716 counties outside New Mexico accounted for at least one record with stress data. An average of 1.83 stress factors (85,967 factors for 46,997 families) were recorded for all records from the 18 states which had family stress data.

County Group Comparisons

Child Maltreatment

Maltreatment information from the American Humane Association was linked with environmental data from the Area Resource File for each of the 944 study counties to examine the relationships between variables in the two respective data sets.   See Table 4.1 to examine the relationships.   The average county rate of reported maltreatment was 7.23 per 1,000 children. The highest incidence recorded among the counties was 73.2 per 1,000 children in Steuben County, Indiana.   Counties with fewer than 50,000 residents averaged the fewest number of reports, 6.66, but as previously noted, their rates were the most variant with a standard deviation of 6.0 vs. 4.9 for the 248 counties with populations of at least 50,000.   An analysis of variance indicated very significant county group differences F (2, 941) = 213.56, p < .001.   The Scheffe multiple group comparison test revealed the rate for the least populated counties to be significantly less than that for each of the two sets of counties with greater populations.

Neglect was much more prevalent than either of the other two major types of child maltreatment with a reported rate of 5.60 per 1,000 children. Its standard deviation was also relatively large; 5.97.   As with all reports of mistreatment, much greater variability was observed for rates of child neglect among the least populated counties.   The standard deviation for the reported rate of neglect was 6.49 there vs. 4.22 for the other two county groups combined.   Physical abuse was the only specific form of child mistreatment which significantly differed by population category of the counties F (2, 813) =   10.25, p <   .001.   The Scheffe multiple range test determined the difference between the mean of 1.03 physical abuse reports per 1,000 children for counties with fewer than 50,000 residents vs. 1.55 for counties inhabited by 50,000 to 100,000 persons and 1.52 per 1,000 children for counties with more than 100,000 residents to be significant at the .05 level.

Sexual abuse accounted for the smallest proportion of reports of the three most frequently reported types of child mistreatment in 1980, .52 per 1,000 children with a standard deviation of .64.   However, this relationship of relative incidence has been shifting since 1980 with disproportionately large annual increases in the number of sexual abuse reports. Although the report rates for the three categories were similar, the standard deviation of that rate among the 696 least populated counties was almost twice that for counties with more than 50,000 inhabitants (.71 vs. .37).

Socioeconomic Status

Significance tests for county group differences on each of the 33 independent variables are depicted in Table 4.1.   The economic standing and educational attainment of residents of counties with more than 100,000 population exceeded significantly that of persons living in   counties with fewer inhabitants.   The populations of counties with less than 50,000 residents were also significantly socioeconomically disadvantaged compared

Table 4.1. Comparisons Between Counties Grouped by Population on 33 Environmental Variables

Variables	Mean for Counties Pop Under 50,000 *(Group 1)	Mean for Counties Pop 50,000-99,999 *(Group 2)	Mean for Counties Pop 100,000+ *(Group 3)	F Ratio	Sig. of F	Significant Group * Differences
Per capita income	7275	7991	9398	116.95	<.001	1,2 1,3 2,3
Median family income	15670	18575	20967	197.24	<.001	1,2 1,3 2,3
Percent of families below poverty level	12.8	9.7	8.1	47.58	<.001	1,2 1,3
Percent of children below poverty level	18.4	14.5	13.1	29.23	<.001	1,2 1,3
Median home value	30852	40647	46278	139.75	<.001	1,2 1,3 2,3
Percent of persons 16+ years in labor force unemployed	7.8	8.2	7.8	.77	n.s.	none
Percent of persons receiving Aid to Families with Dependent Children	3.3	3.8	4.3	4.39	.013	1,3
Median school years for persons 25+ years	12.0	12.3	12.4	34.25	<.001	1,2 1,3
Percent of persons 25+ years with less than 9 years school	25.3	20.1	16.2	84.57	<.001	1,2 1,3 2,3
Percent of persons 25+ years with high school or more	59.6	64.8	68.6	56.05	<.001	1,2 1,3 2,3
Percent of families with female head	6.9	8.5	10.0	66.01	<.001	1,2 1,3 2,3
Percent of females divorced	4.4	5.7	6.8	117.28	<.001	1,2 1,3 2,3
Divorces per 1000 adults	5.8	7.3	7.3	18.55	<.001	1,2 1,3
Percent of non-married couple families	13.1	14.9	17.8	65.42	<.001	1,2 1,3 2,3
Percent of births to teens	16.3	15.5	13.9	9.30	<.001	1,3
Births per 1000 persons	16.4	17.1	15.8	5.97	.003	2,3

Variable				F	p	Significant pairs
Deaths per 1000 persons	10.1	8.0	8.1	66.12	<.001	1,2 1,3
Natural increase in population 1970-1975 as percent of 1980 population.	1.9	3.9	3.7	87.57	<.001	1,2 1,3
Natural change in population 1970-1975 as percent of 1980 population.	2.3	3.9	3.7	81.82	<.001	1,2 1,3
Net in-migration 1970-1975 as percent of 1980 population.	2.1	3.0	.8	2.84	n.s.	none
Net migration 1970-1975 as percent of 1980 population.	5.6	5.2	4.6	2.46	n.s.	none
Percent of persons occupying housing unit with telephone	90.9	91.2	94.4	16.11	<.001	1,3 2,3
Percent of households with 6+ persons . .	5.9	6.6	5.6	5.62	.004	1,2 2,3
Percent of births low birthweight	5.8	6.2	6.6	5.81	.003	1,3
Crimes per 1000 persons	23.4	38.1	57.1	166.43	<.001	1,2 1,3 2,3
Non-property crimes per 1000 persons. . .	1.4	2.5	4.9	69.03	<.001	1,2 1,3 2,3
Percent of adults 45+ minutes from work .	4.6	5.0	5.5	3.54	.029	1,3
Percent of adults working outside county of residence	22.0	23.2	20.3	1.03	n.s.	none
Percent of children racial minority . . .	11.1	13.4	16.7	4.60	.010	1,3
Population per square mile.	34.3	111.6	1890.7	27.25	<.001	1,3 2,3
Census population	19185	70788	372557	279.22	<.001	1,2 1,3 2,3
Natural increase in population 1970-1975	457	2791	12854	262.28	<.001	1,2 1,3 2,3
Net migration 1970-1975	443	2065	-5253	7.95	<.001	1,3 2,3

Note: Pairs of groups significantly different at the .05 level determined by the Scheffe Multiple Range Test Procedure.

with the residents of counties with 50,000 to 100,000 people. These comparisons were established for economic status primarily by examining the following variables:

(1) per capita income
(2) median family income
(3) percent of families below poverty level
(4) percent of children below poverty level
(5) median home value
(6) percent of persons 16+ years in labor force unemployed
(7) percent of persons receiving Aid to Families with Dependent Children

The finding for the analysis of unemployment rates was not consistent with the general socioeconomic pattern. There was little variation in rates between county groups. Unemployment is a circumstance that may be very short-lived and can be experienced briefly by affluent individuals. But the percentage of the population receiving benefits from the Aid to Families with Dependent Children Program (AFDC) was inversely related in rank order to income and poverty level by county population category. Whereas the highest proportion of poor families was found in the less populated counties, beneficiaries of the AFDC program tended to reside in the largest counties (4.27 percent). A greater percentage of persons in counties with 50,000 to 100,000 inhabitants (3.85 percent) also received benefits than those in counties with less than 50,000 persons (3.33 percent). Intergroup differences were significant, $F (2, 941) = 4.39$, $p = .012$. The 117 most populated counties and the 696 with the least population were significantly different. It is troubling that perhaps the ineffectiveness of certain departments of social service in certifying persons and families for benefits for which they are eligible or a stigma related to 'welfare' program participation would prevent individuals from receiving aid to which they are legally entitled.

The percentage of children below the poverty level exceeded considerably the percentage of families that were impoverished. An average of 17.2 percent of all children per county were living in poverty. Within the United States, children are proportionally more heavily concentrated among the poor than are the members of any other age group (Duncan, Hill, & Rogers, 1986). Nowhere have children been spared the effects of economic disadvantage. But the harshness of this phenomenon has been most pronounced in small counties. The mean percentage of children in poor families there (18.4 percent) was significantly greater than for counties with 50,000 to 100,000 inhabitants (14.5 percent) or more than 100,000 people (13.1 percent).

An indirect indicator of economic status included in this analysis is the percentage of persons in housing with a telephone. There are other housing characteristic markers available from the results of the national decennial census which are indicative of a more grievous economic situation for a family. Circumstances are clearly more acute for the population living in dwellings without heat or plumbing. But these individuals comprise a very small percentage of the general population. In addition, the lack of access to a telephone seems pertinent to the issue of social isolation, said to be pervasive among families abusive and neglectful of their children. The same hierarchy can be observed for this variable as for most of the others analyzed in assessing economic standing. A larger percentage of persons in counties with huge populations have access to a telephone in their home. Residents of counties with less than 50,000 inhabitants are proportionately more likely to live in a dwelling without this feature usually taken for granted in modern society. The other primary component of socioeconomic status is education. A number of variables pertaining to formal education were included in an analysis employing the same methods as earlier described:

(1) median school years for persons 25+ years old
(2) percent of persons 25+ years with less than 9 years of school
(3) percent of persons 25+ with high school or more.

The results paralleled those obtained for economic status. On all three measures educational attainment varied directly with county population. All between group differences were statistically significant (See Table 4.1). On average, about 4 of every 10 (40.4 percent) adults living in counties with less than 50,000 population had not reached the fundamental plateau of the American education system--graduation from high school.

Family Structure

The deterioration of the structure of the family has been cited as a source of frustration which leads to the mistreatment of children. A core of relevant variables were examined:

(1) percent of families with female head
(2) percent of females divorced
(3) divorces per 1,000 adults
(4) percent of non-married couple families
(5) percent of births to teens

Portrayal of this information by county size appears in Table 4.1. Its contents indicate that on balance, family stability and maintenance of the basic family unit were inversely related to population size. These attributes were particularly characteristic of counties with small populations. The absence of either spouse was much more an exception in sparsely settled counties than in heavily populated ones. The relationship of population to the percentage of female-headed families was very nearly linear. Families headed by a female were less prevalent among the least populated counties.

Much of the blame for disintegration of the contemporary family unit has been attributed to divorce. Thus, the previous two variables can be seen as the product of the percentage of females divorced and the number of divorces per 1,000 adults, both of which also formed a direct statistically significant association with county size.

Adolescent pregnancy has been made the target of a variety of state and federal programs. Birth to teens could almost as properly be classified as a socioeconomic variable, since the cost to society for the care and mainte-nance of the child and young mother is enormous. But because the majority of these births are illegitimate and the young father does not take up cohabitation with mother and child, development of a maladaptive family form is the usual consequence. Teen pregnancy is viewed by many as a problem of the inner city. But Table 4.1 shows this presumption to be invalid. Its incidence was greatest in counties with fewer than 50,000 people. The proportion of births to teens there exceeded statistically significantly that for the most populated counties.

One additional item was not included in the core set of family structure variables. The percent of households with 6+ persons was excluded because non-family members could be included in the Census Bureau definition of members of the household. Households consisting of at least 6 persons were more common in counties of the mid-population range (50,000 to 100,000) than in either of the two extreme population categories. These households which were rare to counties of any specified size, were more prevalent among counties with less than 50,000 people than among those with populations in excess of 100,000. The importance of the influence of this household configuration on child maltreatment rates is discussed later. It will be shown to represent the presence of others who increase family stability rather than simply overcrowding.

Population Change

Aspects of the population and factors with the potential to reshape it over time are also profiled in Table 4.1. Table 4.1 contains the results of an assessment of the relationship of these variables to county population. The highest birth rates were found in mid-population-range counties and statistically significantly exceeded those for the 117 most populated counties. The crude mortality rate of the 696 counties in which fewer than 50,000 persons resided exceeded substantially that for the groups of counties with more population. The combination of birth and death rates manifest themselves in natural population increases which along with migration dictate changes in the general population. The natural increase in already sparsely settled counties lagged dramatically compared with that for counties with greater population. Group differences in both the net migration and the absolute value of the difference between in- and out- migration as a percentage of the 1980 population approached but did not attain statistical significance. Migration data were applicable to a six-year period that began in 1970. Therefore, this information represents an earlier trend of population movement which could easily have ceased or been altered by 1980, the year for which child maltreatment data were available.

Other Variables

Two residual categories of variables also appear in Table 4.1. Although none of the items in the first residual category may fit neatly into the three principal variable categories that have been discussed, each represents an event or circumstance which has the potential to produce stress:

(1) percent of persons occupying housing unit with telephone
(2) percent of households with 6+ persons
(3) percent of births low birth weight
(4) crimes per 1000 persons
(5) non-property crimes per 1000 persons
(6) percent of adults 45+ minutes from workplace
(7) percent of adults working outside county of residence
(8) percent of children racial minority
(9) population per square mile

The percent of low birth weight births, excessive travel time to the workplace, the crime rate and non-property (including violent) crime rate all varied directly with county population, although differences were only significant between the least vs. the most populated county groups for the first two variables. Differences were very significant between all county groups for both the general and non-property crime rates. There was no relationship between county group and working outside the county in which the worker resided.

Another variable, percentage of children who are members of ethnic minorities, which has often been hypothesized to be linked with rates of child maltreatment, pertains to the composition rather than the size of the population. Ethnic minorities were found more heavily concentrated in counties with more than 100,000 inhabitants.

The second category pertains to the general population, but unlike all other variables, its items do not represent rates or percentages:

(1) census population
(2) natural increase in population
(3) net migration

Environmental Variable Correlation with Child Maltreatment Rules

Simple correlation coefficients and the level of significance of the relationships of these variables with child maltreatment and its three most prevalent forms are presented in Tables 4.2, 4.3, 4.4, 4.5, and 4.6. These are zero-order correlations uncontrolled for the effects of other variables. But the ultimate application for these items is their inclusion in multiple regression equations which

> can be viewed both as a means of evaluating the overall contribution
> of the independent variables and as a means of evaluating the contri-
> bution of a particular independent variable with the influence of other
> independent variables controlled. (Nie et al., 1975, p. 332)

The potential of the variable set can be seen from the fact that only two of the items did not have a significant association with at least one of the four dependent variables for the analysis of all counties. The nature and number of relationships differed across counties grouped by population. Especially evident is the association of socioeconomic variables with rates of child neglect. But family structure items were the most useful variable set in explaining all forms of maltreatment across each county grouping. Family configuration was particularly more powerful than socioeconomic status in its association with physical abuse rates. Rates of sexual abuse exhibited fewer relationships with the environmental variables that were consistent across county population categories.

Multiple Regression of Rates of
Reported Child Maltreatment on
Environmental Variables

The 33 independent variables explained about one-third (R Square = .341) of the total variance in rates of reported maltreatment throughout the 944 counties. Table 4.7 portrays the result of forced entry regression using all of the 33 variables to account for variance in the rates of child mistreatment. The standard error of the estimate was 4.83. Since it is more than half the magnitude of the actual rate, it is clearly unacceptably high for purposes of fine tuning the distribution of child protection worker personnel with the responsibility for response to reports of the various types of child mistreatment. The equation derived for the 696 counties with less than 50,000 people was similar in its effectiveness to account for variation in rates of reported child mistreatment (R Square = .335, Standard Error = 5.07). These analyses are sensitive to variations in the size of the units of analysis. The explanatory power of the independent variables was much greater for counties with more than 50,000 inhabitants (see Table 4.7). But even among the two larger population categories, there is good reason to treat each separately in attempting to account for abuse and neglect rates. There was not a single form of maltreatment for which the variance explained for the 248 counties of the combined categories exceeded that for either of the categories of counties analyzed separately. Therefore, crude aggregation of geographic units vastly different in population will obscure useful relationships among variables. Inclusion of counties in which a small number of events--in this case, child maltreatment--take place will have essentially the same effect. Analysts must be resigned to these limitations.

In each of the two categories of larger counties (populations of 50,000-99,999 and 100,000+), the associations between maltreatment rates and the sets of independent variables were strong. These two categories, in which the strength of the relationship between maltreatment and the 33 social and economic variables was greatest, comprise about 80 percent of the total population of the 18 states. For both neglect and physical abuse, more than half of the variance in rates could be explained, almost two-thirds in the largest county population category. Because the standard error for all associations was large in comparison with the magnitude of the rate, the products of these regression equations are too imprecise to be used as a basis for the allocation of personnel to handle cases brought to the attention of departments of social services during a single fiscal or calendar year. But for the purpose of equitable apportionment of child protection personnel resources among counties, administrators would do much better with these insights than without them.

Table 4.2. Simple Correlations Between Child Maltreatment Rates and 33 Environmental Variables for all Counties

Variables	All forms		Neglect		Phys abuse		Sexual abuse	
	r	p-value	r	p-value	r	p-value	r	p-value
Per capita income	-.079	.018	-.203	<.001	-.040	n.s.	-.108	.001
Median family income.	-.033	n.s.	-.202	<.001	.025	n.s.	-.028	n.s.
Percent of families below poverty level . .	-.029	n.s.	.188	<.001	.041	n.s.	.006	n.s.
Percent of children below poverty level . .	-.004	n.s.	.194	<.001	.051	n.s.	.009	n.s.
Median home value	-.039	n.s.	-.156	<.001	.061	n.s.	.025	n.s.
Percent of persons 16+ years in labor force unemployed.	.356	<.001	.264	<.001	.186	<.001	.223	<.001
Percent of persons receiving Aid to Families with Dependent Children.	.154	<.001	.169	<.001	.114	.002	.154	<.001
Median school years for persons 25+ years	-.000	n.s.	-.220	<.001	-.065	n.s.	-.077	.022
Percent of persons 25+ years with less than 9 years school.	-.118	<.001	.159	<.001	-.053	n.s.	-.019	n.s.
Percent of persons 25+ years with high school or more	-.034	n.s.	-.292	<.001	-.073	.044	-.055	n.s.
Percent of families with female head.	.181	<.001	.231	<.001	.255	<.001	.136	<.001
Percent of females divorced	.383	<.001	.175	<.001	.260	<.001	.121	<.001
Divorces per 1000 adults.	.346	<.001	.218	<.001	.247	<.001	.143	<.001
Percent of non-married couple families.	.169	<.001	.186	<.001	.227	<.001	.104	.002
Percent of births to teens.	.241	<.001	.370	<.001	.249	<.001	.154	<.001

Births per 1000 persons	-.105	.002	.004	n.s.	.076	.037	.041	n.s.
Deaths per 1000 persons	.004	n.s.	.071	.033	-.052	n.s.	-.038	n.s.
Natural increase in population 1970-1975 as percent of 1980 population.	.074	.027	.021	n.s.	.180	<.001	.083	.014
Natural change in population 1970-1975 as percent of 1980 population.	.043	n.s.	.027	n.s.	.164	<.001	.059	n.s.
Net in-migration 1970-1975 as percent of 1980 population.	.183	<.001	.139	<.001	.202	n.s.	.122	<.001
Net migration 1970-1975 as percent of 1980 population.	.142	<.001	.153	<.001	.058	n.s.	.070	.037
Percent of persons occupying housing unit with telephone	-.088	.009	-.243	<.001	-.192	<.001	-.059	n.s.
Percent of households with 6+ persons	-.143	<.001	-.027	n.s.	-.044	n.s.	.021	n.s.
Percent of births low birthweight	.129	<.001	.177	<.001	.143	<.001	.122	<.001
Crimes per 1000 persons	.267	<.001	.094	.005	.148	<.001	.145	<.001
Non-property crimes per 1000 persons.	.156	<.001	.132	<.001	.555	<.001	.097	.004
Percent of adults 45+ minutes from work	.065	n.s.	.065	n.s.	.090	.013	.042	n.s.
Percent of adults working outside county of residence	-.035	n.s.	-.020	n.s.	-.015	n.s.	.041	n.s.
Percent of children racial minority	-.025	n.s.	.119	<.001	.163	<.001	.027	n.s.
Population per square mile.	.059	n.s.	-.008	n.s.	.013	n.s.	-.026	n.s.
Census population.	.081	.016	-.042	n.s.	.075	.039	-.000	n.s.
Natural increase in population 1970-1975	.063	n.s.	-.035	n.s.	.098	.007	.022	n.s.
Net migration 1970-1975	-.025	n.s.	-.009	n.s.	-.001	n.s.	.019	n.s.

Table 4.3. Simple Correlations Between Child Maltreatment Rates and 33 Environmental Variables for Counties with Population Under 50,000

Variables	All forms		Neglect		Phys abuse		Sexual abuse	
	r	p-value	r	p-value	r	p-value	r	p-value
Per capita income	-.168	<.001	-.194	<.001	-.106	.012	-.153	<.001
Median family income.	-.088	.026	-.184	<.001	-.009	n.s.	-.046	n.s.
Percent of families below poverty level . .	.000	n.s.	.158	<.001	.068	n.s.	.020	n.s.
Percent of children below poverty level . .	.005	n.s.	.164	<.001	.064	n.s.	.021	n.s.
Median home value	-.040	n.s.	-.118	.003	.029	n.s.	.027	n.s.
Percent of persons 16+ years in labor force unemployed.	.368	<.001	.277	<.001	.189	<.001	.249	<.001
Percent of persons receiving Aid to Families with Dependent Children. . . .	.198	<.001	.242	<.001	.162	<.001	.217	<.001
Median school years for persons 25+ years .	-.049	n.s.	-.207	<.001	-.092	.029	-.089	.024
Percent of persons 25+ years with less than 9 years school.	-.067	n.s.	.131	.001	-.031	n.s.	-.016	n.s.
Percent of persons 25+ years with high school or more.	-.094	.017	-.278	<.001	-.104	.014	-.070	n.s.
Percent of families with female head. . .	.162	<.001	.264	<.001	.245	<.001	.166	<.001
Percent of females divorced	.369	<.001	.230	<.001	.233	<.001	.120	.002
Divorces per 1000 adults.	.328	<.001	-.095	.013	.216	<.001	-.095	.013
Percent of non-married couple families. . .	.135	.001	.223	<.001	.226	<.001	.138	<.001
Percent of births to teens.	.262	<.001	.328	<.001	.233	<.001	.149	<.001

Variable								
Births per 1000 persons	-.088	.025	-.046	n.s.	.039	n.s.	.025	n.s.
Deaths per 1000 persons	.013	n.s.	.056	n.s.	-.010	n.s.	-.030	n.s.
Natural increase in population 1970-1975 as percent of 1980 population	.075	n.s.	.034	n.s.	.160	<.001	.079	.046
Natural change in population 1970-1975 as percent of 1980 population	.046	n.s.	.043	n.s.	.148	<.001	.051	n.s.
Net in-migration 1970-1975 as percent of 1980 population	.257	<.001	.184	<.001	.030	n.s.	.150	<.001
Net migration 1970-1975 as percent of 1980 population	.177	<.001	.164	<.001	.080	n.s.	.087	.027
Percent of persons occupying housing unit with telephone	-.142	<.001	-.242	<.001	-.233	<.001	-.081	.038
Percent of households with 6+ persons	-.100	.011	-.020	n.s.	.074	n.s.	.040	n.s.
Percent of births low birthweight	.118	.003	.156	<.001	.110	.009	.132	.001
Crimes per 1000 persons	.329	<.001	.170	<.001	.116	.006	.207	<.001
Non-property crimes per 1000 persons	.220	<.001	.237	<.001	.207	<.001	.206	<.001
Percent of adults 45+ minutes from work	.139	<.001	.125	.001	.163	<.001	.107	.006
Percent of adults working outside county of residence	.033	n.s.	.020	n.s.	.048	n.s.	.093	.018
Percent of children racial minority	-.026	n.s.	.106	.007	.154	<.001	.033	n.s.
Population per square mile	.016	n.s.	-.010	n.s.	.057	n.s.	.009	n.s.
Census population	.191	<.001	.100	.011	.166	<.001	.115	.003
Natural increase in population 1970-1975	.120	.002	.075	n.s.	.164	<.001	.079	.045
Net migration 1970-1975	.198	<.001	.098	.013	.030	n.s.	.125	.001

Table 4.4. Simple Correlations Between Child Maltreatment Rates and 33 Environmental Variables for Counties with Population 50,000-99,000

Variables	All forms r	p-value	Neglect r	p-value	Phys abuse r	p-value	Sexual abuse r	p-value
Per capita income	-.118	n.s.	-.314	<.001	-.187	n.s.	-.080	n.s.
Median family income	-.258	.003	-.342	<.001	-.242	.012	-.113	n.s.
Percent of families below poverty level	-.007	n.s.	.266	.002	.129	n.s.	-.023	n.s.
Percent of children below poverty level	.053	n.s.	.263	.002	.151	n.s.	-.024	n.s.
Median home value	-.382	<.001	-.306	<.001	-.193	.048	-.078	n.s.
Percent of persons 16+ years in labor force unemployed	.278	.001	.159	n.s.	.121	n.s.	.097	n.s.
Percent of persons receiving Aid to Families with Dependent Children	.044	n.s.	.037	n.s.	-.020	n.s.	.009	n.s.
Median school years for persons 25+ years	-.006	n.s.	-.346	<.001	-.261	.007	-.112	n.s.
Percent of persons 25+ years with less than 9 years school	-.094	n.s.	.264	.002	.193	.047	.033	n.s.
Percent of persons 25+ years with high school or more	-.048	n.s.	-.348	<.001	-.280	.004	-.052	n.s.
Percent of families with female head	-.063	n.s.	.140	n.s.	.035	n.s.	-.120	n.s.
Percent of females divorced	.301	<.001	.082	n.s.	.009	n.s.	.037	n.s.
Divorces per 1000 adults	.347	<.001	.202	.021	.162	n.s.	.177	.043
Percent of non-married couple families	-.030	n.s.	.064	n.s.	-.041	n.s.	-.175	.047
Percent of births to teens	.282	.001	.517	<.001	.465	<.001	.163	n.s.

Births per 1000 persons	-.222	.011	.100	r.s.	.124	n.s.	.005	n.s.
Deaths per 1000 persons	.317	<.001	.141	r.s.	.059	n.s.	.083	n.s.
Natural increase in population 1970-1975 as percent of 1980 population	-.312	<.001	-.098	n.s.	-.085	n.s.	-.107	n.s.
Natural change in population 1970-1975 as percent of 1980 population	-.308	<.001	-.095	n.s.	-.084	n.s.	-.107	n.s.
Net in-migration 1970-1975 as percent of 1980 population	.037	n.s.	-.041	n.s.	-.148	n.s.	-.023	n.s.
Net migration 1970-1975 as percent of 1980 population	.072	n.s.	.112	n.s.	-.011	n.s.	-.004	n.s.
Percent of persons occupying housing unit with telephone	.059	n.s.	-.167	n.s.	-.103	n.s.	.067	n.s.
Percent of households with 6+ persons	-.348	<.001	-.106	n.s.	-.097	n.s.	-.124	n.s.
Percent of births low birthweight	.079	n.s.	.281	.001	.270	.005	-.071	n.s.
Crimes per 1000 persons	.070	n.s.	-.024	n.s.	-.060	n.s.	-.010	n.s.
Non-property crimes per 1000 persons	-.015	n.s.	.203	.021	.184	n.s.	-.032	n.s.
Percent of adults 45+ minutes from work	-.171	n.s.	-.033	n.s.	-.035	n.s.	-.067	n.s.
Percent of adults working outside county of residence	-.170	n.s.	-.111	n.s.	-.041	n.s.	-.034	n.s.
Percent of children racial minority	-.222	.011	.083	n.s.	.020	n.s.	-.134	n.s.
Population per square mile	-.122	n.s.	-.152	n.s.	-.122	n.s.	-.102	n.s.
Census population	-.028	n.s.	-.125	n.s.	-.086	n.s.	-.037	n.s.
Natural increase in population 1970-1975	-.293	.001	-.133	n.s.	-.105	n.s.	-.119	n.s.
Net migration 1970-1975	.044	n.s.	-.041	n.s.	-.101	n.s.	-.004	n.s.

Table 4.5. Simple Correlations Between Child Maltreatment Rates and 33 Environmental Variables for Counties with Population 100,000+

Variables	All forms r	All forms p-value	Neglect r	Neglect p-value	Phys abuse r	Phys abuse p-value	Sexual abuse r	Sexual abuse p-value
Per capita income	-.077	n.s.	-.326	<.001	-.068	n.s.	-.140	n.s.
Median family income	-.261	.005	-.432	<.001	-.195	n.s.	-.141	n.s.
Percent of families below poverty level	.223	.016	.504	<.001	.263	.013	.072	n.s.
Percent of children below poverty level	.256	.005	.482	<.001	.250	.019	.048	n.s.
Median home value	-.279	.002	-.367	<.001	-.022	n.s.	-.045	n.s.
Percent of persons 16+ years in labor force unemployed	.348	<.001	.256	.005	.205	n.s.	.023	n.s.
Percent of persons receiving Aid to Families with Dependent Children	.300	.001	.284	.002	.045	n.s.	-.102	n.s.
Median school years for persons 25+ years	-.032	n.s.	-.412	<.001	-.189	n.s.	-.193	.037
Percent of persons 25+ years with less than 9 years school	-.041	n.s.	.418	<.001	.161	n.s.	.168	n.s.
Percent of persons 25+ years with high school or more	-.078	n.s.	-.514	<.001	-.240	.024	-.157	n.s.
Percent of families with female head	.233	.012	.409	<.001	.205	n.s.	-.009	n.s.
Percent of females divorced	.438	<.001	.286	.002	.397	<.001	.218	.018
Divorces per 1000 adults	.319	<.001	.232	.012	.406	<.001	.232	.012
Percent of non-married couple families	.287	.002	.356	<.001	.197	n.s.	-.024	n.s.
Percent of births to teens	.278	.002	.721	<.001	.547	<.001	.389	<.001

Births per 1000 persons	-.131	n.s.	.325	<.001	.385	<.001	.383	<.001
Deaths per 1000 persons	.286	.002	.189	.041	.022	n.s.	-.076	n.s.
Natural increase in population 1970-1975 as percent of 1980 population.	-.111	n.s.	.195	.036	.223	.037	.290	.002
Natural change in population 1970-1975 as percent of 1980 population.	-.103	n.s.	.201	.030	.228	.032	.290	.002
Net in-migration 1970-1975 as percent of 1980 population.	-.292	.001	-.200	.031	-.111	n.s.	-.049	n.s.
Net migration 1970-1975 as percent of 1980 population.	.044	n.s.	.051	n.s.	.012	n.s.	-.009	n.s.
Percent of persons occupying housing unit with telephone	-.186	.045	-.520	<.001	-.409	<.001	-.173	n.s.
Percent of households with 6+ persons	-.318	<.001	-.054	n.s.	-.085	n.s.	.008	n.s.
Percent of births low birthweight	.164	n.s.	.520	<.001	.266	.012	.102	n.s.
Crimes per 1000 persons	.127	n.s.	.196	.035	.153	n.s.	.086	n.s.
Non-property crimes per 1000 persons.	.141	n.s.	.230	.0'2	.130	n.s.	.016	n.s.
Percent of adults 45+ minutes from work.	-.127	n.s.	-.154	n.s.	-.253	.017	-.346	<.001
Percent of adults working outside county of residence	-.275	.003	-.255	.006	-.412	<.001	-.315	.001
Percent of children racial minority	.099	n.s.	.425	<.001	.305	.004	.124	n.s.
Population per square mile.	.150	n.s.	.028	n.s.	-.051	n.s.	-.169	n.s.
Census population	.060	n.s.	-.091	n.s.	-.010	n.s.	-.149	n.s.
Natural increase in population 1970-1975	.010	n.s.	-.044	n.s.	.095	n.s.	.012	n.s.
Net migration 1970-1975	-.136	n.s.	-.108	n.s.	.032	n.s.	.057	n.s.

Table 4.6. Simple Correlations Between Child Maltreatment Rates and 33 Environmental Variables for Counties with Population 50,000+

Variables	All forms		Neglect		Phys abuse		Sexual abuse	
	r	p-value	r	p-value	r	p-value	r	p-value
Per capita income	-.121	n.s.	-.314	<.001	-.116	n.s.	-.083	n.s.
Median family income.	-.262	<.001	-.401	<.001	-.211	.003	-.124	n.s.
Percent of families below poverty level . .	.084	n.s.	.362	<.001	.175	.015	.016	n.s.
Percent of children below poverty level . .	.141	.027	.353	<.001	.191	.008	.008	n.s.
Median home value	-.333	<.001	-.346	<.001	-.113	n.s.	-.064	n.s.
Percent of persons 16+ years in labor force unemployed.	.309	<.001	.203	.001	.154	.034	.066	n.s.
Percent of persons receiving Aid to Families with Dependent Children. . . .	.042	n.s.	.037	n.s.	-.005	n.s.	.007	n.s.
Median school years for persons 25+ years .	-.002	n.s.	-.347	<.001	-.232	.001	-.106	n.s.
Percent of persons 25+ years with less than 9 years school.	-.056	n.s.	.343	<.001	.176	.014	.078	n.s.
Percent of persons 25+ years with high school or more.	-.068	n.s.	-.427	<.001	-.259	<.001	-.087	n.s.
Percent of families with female head. . .	.058	n.s.	.194	.002	.109	n.s.	-.067	n.s.
Percent of females divorced	.322	<.001	.106	n.s.	.176	.014	.109	n.s.
Divorces per 1000 adults.	.326	<.001	.205	.001	.273	<.001	.200	.002
Percent of non-married couple families. .	.111	n.s.	.137	.032	.079	n.s.	-.088	n.s.

	r	p	r	p	r	p	r	p
Percent of births to teens	.286	<.001	.602	<.001	.488	<.001	.256	<.001
Births per 1000 persons	-.173	.006	.190	.003	.196	.006	.116	n.s.
Deaths per 1000 persons	.301	<.001	.151	.017	.043	n.s.	.014	n.s.
Natural increase in population 1970-1975 as percent of 1980 population	-.238	<.001	.004	n.s.	.015	n.s.	.031	n.s.
Natural change in population 1970-1975 as percent of 1980 population	-.233	<.001	.007	n.s.	.017	n.s.	.029	n.s.
Net in-migration 1970-1975 as percent of 1980 population	-.084	n.s.	-.070	n.s.	-.129	n.s.	-.030	n.s.
Net migration 1970-1975 as percent of 1980 population	.066	n.s.	.101	n.s.	-.002	n.s.	-.005	n.s.
Percent of persons occupying housing unit with telephone	-.014	n.s.	-.265	<.001	-.153	.034	.003	n.s.
Percent of households with 6+ persons	-.310	<.001	-.055	n.s.	-.086	n.s.	-.089	n.s.
Percent of births low birthweight	.104	n.s.	.340	<.001	.264	<.001	-.002	n.s.
Crimes per 1000 persons	.068	n.s.	.030	n.s.	.057	n.s.	.035	n.s.
Non-property crimes per 1000 persons	.064	n.s.	.134	.035	.111	n.s.	-.0025	n.s.
Percent of adults 45+ minutes from work	-.145	.023	-.095	n.s.	-.144	.045	-.209	.001
Percent of adults working outside county of residence	-.208	.001	-.151	.018	-.200	.005	-.154	.016
Percent of children racial minority	-.098	n.s.	.191	.003	.133	n.s.	-.030	n.s.
Population per square mile	.079	n.s.	-.014	n.s.	-.034	n.s.	-.110	n.s.
Census population	.004	n.s.	-.122	n.s.	-.014	n.s.	-.094	n.s.
Natural increase in population 1970-1975	-.041	n.s.	-.100	n.s.	.037	n.s.	-.011	n.s.
Net migration 1970-1975	-.071	n.s.	-.045	n.s.	.011	n.s.	.037	n.s.

TABLE 4.7. Regression of Rates of Reported Child Maltreatment on 33 Environmental Variables

Type of Maltreatment	All Counties (n=944)	Counties with Population Under 50,000 (n=696)	Counties with Population 50,000-99,999 (n=131)	Counties with Population 100,000+ (n=117)	Counties with Population 50,000+ (n=248)
All:					
Multiple R	.58	.58	.80	.70	.70
Multiple R Square	.34	.34	.64	.49	.49
Standard Error	4.83	5.07	3.66	3.72	3.76
Physical Abuse:					
Multiple R	.42	.41	.74	.81	.68
Multiple R Square	.18	.17	.55	.65	.46
Standard Error	1.29	1.37	.96	.75	.89
Neglect:					
Multiple R	.51	.51	.78	.80	.74
Multiple R Square	.26	.26	.61	.64	.54
Standard Error	5.14	5.63	3.39	2.48	3.07
Sexual Abuse:					
Multiple R	.35	.39	.59	.68	.49
Multiple R Square	.12	.15	.35	.46	.24
Standard Error	.61	.68	.36	.29	.34

The value of the range of environmental variables employed in the analysis can be discerned from the content of Tables 4.8 through 4.27. Twenty-one of the variables were significant in accounting for the variance in rates of all reports of maltreatment for at least one of the county population groups. The order of entry of variables into the equations was determined by the percentage of variance they explained not accounted for by variables that had already been entered. This forward stepwise procedure was terminated when F-to-enter for the variables not included in the regression equation was not significant at the .05 level.

In spite of the utility of most of the independent variables, two were clearly the most dominant. 'Percent of birth to teens' was entered first into the equation for child neglect at every population level and was the only independent variable required to explain more than half (51.2 percent) of the variance in neglect rates among the 117 counties with at least 100,000 residents. It was also the most explanatory independent variable in the

TABLE 4.8. Forward Stepwise Regression of Rates of Reported Child Maltreatment on 33 Environmental Variables for All Counties

Variables	Entry Step Number	Multiple R Square	Standard Error
Percent of females divorced.	1	.147	5.39
Percent of persons 16+ years in labor force unemployed	2	.222	5.15
Percent of households with 6+ persons. . .	3	.247	5.07
Percent of births to teens	4	.261	5.02
Crimes per 1000 persons.	5	.278	4.97
Natural increase in population 1970-1975 .	6	.283	4.95
Divorces per 1000 adults	7	.287	4.94
Median home value.	8	.291	4.93
Net in-migration 1970-1975 as percent of 1980 population	9	.295	4.92
Census population.	10	.301	4.90
Natural increase in population 1970-1975 as percent of 1980 population.	11	.307	4.88
Non-property crimes per 1000 persons . . .	12	.311	4.87
Percent of adults 45+ minutes from work. .	13	.314	4.87

TABLE 4.9. Forward Stepwise Regression of Rates of Reported Child Maltreatment on 33 Environmental Variables for Counties with Population Under 50,000

Variables	Entry Step Number	Multiple R Square	Standard Error
Percent of females divorced.	1	.135	5.63
Percent of persons 16+ years in labor force unemployed.	2	.210	5.39
Crimes per 1000 persons.	3	.241	5.28
Percent of households with 6+ persons. . .	4	.259	5.23
Percent of births to teens	5	.280	5.15
Divorces per 1000 adults	6	.285	5.14
Median home value.	7	.290	5.13
Net migration 1970-1975.	8	.296	5.11
Natural increase in population 1970-1975 as percent of 1980 population.	9	.301	5.10
Percent of adults 45+ minutes from work. .	10	.306	5.08

56

TABLE 4.10. Forward Stepwise Regression of Rates of Reported Child Maltreatment on 33 Environmental Variables for Counties with Population 50,000-99,999

Variables	Entry Step Number	Multiple R Square	Standard Error
Median home value.	1	.146	4.93
Percent of households with 6+ persons. . .	2	.282	4.54
Divorces per 1000 adults	3	.359	4.30
Percent of persons receiving Aid to Families with Dependent Children	4	.426	4.09
Net migration 1970-1975 as percent of 1980 population	5	.463	3.97
Population per square mile	6	.495	3.87
Percent of persons 16+ years in labor force unemployed.	7	.533	3.73

TABLE 4.11. Forward Stepwise Regression of Rates of Reported Child Maltreatment on 33 Environmental Variables for Counties with Population 100,000+

Variables	Entry Step Number	Multiple R Square	Standard Error
Percent of females divorced.	1	.186	3.99
Median home value.	2	.273	3.79
Births per 1000 persons.	3	.332	3.65
Percent of families below poverty level. .	4	.367	3.57
Percent of persons 16+ years in labor force unemployed.	5	.393	3.51

TABLE 4.12. Forward Stepwise Regression of Rates of Reported Child Maltreatment on 33 Environmental Variables for Counties with Population 50,000+

Variables	Entry Step Number	Multiple R Square	Standard Error
Median home value.	1	.108	4.64
Percent of females divorced.	2	.236	4.31
Natural increase in population 1970-1975 as percent of 1980 population.	3	.283	4.18
Percent of persons 16+ years in labor force unemployed.	4	.314	4.10
Divorces per 1000 adults	5	.350	4.00
Percent of households with 6+ persons.	6	.370	3.94
Percent of children below poverty level.	7	.416	3.80
Percent of persons 25+ years with high school or more.	8	.433	3.76
Percent of persons receiving Aid to Families with Dependent Children	9	.445	3.73
Percent of births to teens	10	.455	3.70

TABLE 4.13. Forward Stepwise Regression of Rates of Reported Child Neglect on 33 Environmental Variables for All Counties

Variables	Entry Step Number	Multiple R Square	Standard Error
Percent of births to teens	1	.132	5.46
Percent of persons 16+ years in labor force unemployed.	2	.156	5.39
Percent of households with 6+ persons.	3	.176	5.33
Net migration 1970-1975 as percent of 1980 population.	4	.189	5.29
Percent of families with female head	5	.201	5.25
Percent of persons 25+ years with high school or more.	6	.212	5.22
Percent of persons 25+ years with less than 9 years school	7	.220	5.19
Percent of adults working outside county of residence.	8	.228	5.17
Net in-migration 1970-1975 as percent of 1980 population	9	.236	5.15
Natural change in population 1970-1975 as percent of 1980 population.	10	.241	5.13

TABLE 4.14. Forward Stepwise Regression of Rates of Reported Child Neglect on 33 Environmental Variables for Counties with Population Under 50,000

Variables	Entry Step Number	Multiple R Square	Standard Error
Percent of births to teens	1	.103	6.05
Net in-migration 1970-1975 as percent of 1980 population	2	.136	5.94
Non-property crimes per 1000 persons . . .	3	.155	5.88
Percent of persons 16+ years in labor force unemployed.	4	.170	5.83
Percent of households with 6+ persons. . .	5	.188	5.77
Percent of persons 25+ years with high school or more.	6	.205	5.72
Percent of families with female head . . .	7	.217	5.68
Percent of persons 25+ years with less than 9 years school	8	.223	5.66
Percent of adults working outside county of residence.	9	.230	5.64

TABLE 4.15. Forward Stepwise Regression of Rates of Reported Child Neglect on 33 Environmental Variables for Counties with Population 50,000-99,999

Variables	Entry Step Number	Multiple R Square	Standard Error
Percent of births to teens	1	.267	4.06
Percent of households with 6+ persons. . .	2	.326	3.91
Percent of families below poverty level. .	3	.362	3.82
Percent of non-married couple families . .	4	.428	3.63

TABLE 4.16. Forward Stepwise Regression of Rates of Reported Child Neglect on 33 Environmental Variables for Counties with Population 100,000+

Variables	Entry Step Number	Multiple R Square	Standard Error
Percent of births to teens	1	.519	2.43

TABLE 4.17. Forward Stepwise Regression of Rates of Reported Child Neglect on 33 Environmental Variables for Counties with Population 50,000+

Variables	Entry Step Number	Multiple R Square	Standard Error
Percent of births to teens	1	.362	3.39
Percent of households with 6+ persons. . .	2	.397	3.30
Percent of families below poverty level. .	3	.411	3.27
Percent of non-married couple families . .	4	.445	3.18

TABLE 4.18. Forward Stepwise Regression of Rates of Reported Child Physical Abuse on 33 Environmental Variables for All Counties

Variables	Entry Step Number	Multiple R Square	Standard Error
Percent of females divorced.	1	.067	1.35
Percent of births to teens	2	.099	1.33
Natural increase in population 1970-1975 as percent of 1980 population.	3	.108	1.32

60

TABLE 4.19. Forward Stepwise Regression of Rates of Reported Child Physical Abuse on 33 Environmental Variables for Counties with Population Under 50,000

Variables	Entry Step Number	Multiple R Square	Standard Error
Percent of families with female head . . .	1	.060	1.42
Divorces per 1000 adults	2	.080	1.40
Percent of adults 45+ minutes from work. .	3	.089	1.40
Non-property crimes per 1000 persons . . .	4	.096	1.39

TABLE 4.20. Forward Stepwise Regression of Rates of Reported Child Physical Abuse on 33 Environmental Variables for Counties with Population 50,000-99,999

Variables	Entry Step Number	Multiple R Square	Standard Error
Percent of births to teens	1	.216	1.05
Percent of families with female head . . .	2	.285	1.01
Net in-migration 1970-1975 as percent of 1980 population	3	.317	.99
Net migration 1970-1975.	4	.354	.97

TABLE 4.21. Forward Stepwise Regression of Rates of Reported Child Physical Abuse on 33 Environmental Variables for Counties with Population 100,000+

Variables	Entry Step Number	Multiple R Square	Standard Error
Percent of births to teens	1	.299	.86
Percent of adults working outside county of residence.	2	.355	.83
Median home value.	3	.408	.80

TABLE 4.22. Forward Stepwise Regression of Rates of Reported Child Physical Abuse on 33 Environmental Variables for Counties with Population 50,000+

Variables	Entry Step Number	Multiple R Square	Standard Error
Percent of births to teens	1	.238	.97
Percent of households with 6+ persons. . .	2	.272	.95
Births per 1000 persons.	3	.295	.94

TABLE 4.23. Forward Stepwise Regression of Rates of Reported Child Sexual Abuse on 33 Environmental Variables for All Counties

Variables	Entry Step Number	Multiple R Square	Standard Error
Percent of persons 16+ years in labor force unemployed.	1	.050	.63
Crimes per 1000 persons.	2	.063	.62
Percent of births to teens	3	.072	.62
Net in-migration 1970-1975 as percent of 1980 population	4	.080	.62

TABLE 4.24. Forward Stepwise Regression of Rates of Reported Child Sexual Abuse on 33 Environmental Variables for Counties with Population Under 50,000

Variables	Entry Step Number	Multiple R Square	Standard Error
Percent of persons 16+ years in labor force unemployed.	1	.062	.70
Non-property crimes per 1000 persons . . .	2	.088	.69
Net in-migration 1970-1975 as percent of 1980 population	3	.097	.69

TABLE 4.25. Forward Stepwise Regression of Rates of Reported Child Sexual Abuse on 33 Environmental Variables for Counties with Population 50,000 to 99,999

Variables	Entry Step Number	Multiple R Square	Standard Error
Percent of non-married couple families . .	1	.030	.39
Percent of births to teens	2	.110	.37
Median family income	3	.140	.37

TABLE 4.26. Forward Stepwise Regression of Rates of Reported Child Sexual Abuse on 33 Environmental Variables for Counties with Population 100,000+

Variables	Entry Step Number	Multiple R Square	Standard Error
Births per 1000 persons.	1	.157	.31
Percent of adults 45+ minutes from work. .	2	.227	.30
Percent of births to teens	3	.261	.29
Median home value.	4	.298	.29
Percent of non-married couple families . .	5	.325	.28
Net in-migration 1970-1975 as percent of 1980 population	6	.353	.28

TABLE 4.27. Forward Stepwise Regression of Rates of Reported Child Sexual Abuse on 33 Environmental Variables for Counties with Population 50,000+

Variables	Entry Step Number	Multiple R Square	Standard Error
Percent of births to teens	1	.066	.35
Percent of families with female head . . .	2	.112	.35
Natural increase in population 1970-1975 .	3	.133	.34
Percent of adults 45+ minutes from work. .	4	.154	.34

equation for physical abuse for counties with populations of more than 50,000.

Whereas birth to teens was the most explanatory of child neglect, the 'percent of females divorced' was much more strongly related to general maltreatment rates and to physical abuse than were any of the other environmental items. Because of this strong correlation, it was the first variable to enter the equation for regression with rates of reported mistreatment within counties with more than 100,000 inhabitants and those with less than 50,000, as well as for regression on physical abuse rates among these least populated counties.

Almost one-half of the variance in the maltreatment rates of large counties has been explained. But that explanation required 33 independent variables. Regression was again performed to develop a more efficient equation. But stepwise inclusion was performed in accordance with a predetermined hierarchy among variable sets rather than individual variables to discern between the primary sets of environmental variables: (1) economic, (2) educational and (3) family structural, which are strongest in their associations with child abuse and neglect. Three different patterns of entry were carried out for child maltreatment for each county group. Each of the three blocks was forced to enter first in a separate regression with all four dependent variables. There were twelve procedures in all. The blocks consisted of: (1) economic variables--per capita income, median family income, percent of families below poverty level, percent of children below poverty level, and median home value, (2) educational items--median school years for persons 25+ years old, percentage of persons 25+ years old with less than 9 years'school, and percentage of persons 25+ years old with high school or more, and (3) family structural variables--divorces per 1000 adults, percentage of non-married couple families, percentage of families with a female head and percentage of females divorced (see Table 4.28). It was pointed

TABLE 4.28. Regression of Rates of Reported Child Maltreatment on Economic, Educational and Family Structural Variables

All Maltreatment: R-Squared = .37   Standard Error = 3.69

Block	R-Squared when Entered First	Standard Error when Entered First
Economic	.16	4.14
Educational	.12	4.20
Family Structural	.21	3.99

Neglect: R-Squared = .50   Standard Error = 2.61

Block	R-Squared when Entered First	Standard Error when Entered First
Economic	.34	2.89
Educational	.30	2.95
Family Structural	.24	3.09

Physical Abuse: R-Squared = .31   Standard Error = .90

Block	R-Squared when Entered First	Standard Error when Entered First
Economic	.09	.99
Educational	.07	1.01
Family Structural	.22	.92

Sexual Abuse: R-Squared = .25   Standard Error = .31

Block	R-Squared when Entered First	Standard Error when Entered First
Economic	.05	.34
Educational	.04	.33
Family Structural	.07	.33

Economic block consists of:
  (1) per capita income
  (2) median family income
  (3) percent of families below poverty level
  (4) percent of children below poverty level
  (5) median home value
Educational block consists of:
  (1) median school years for persons 25+ years old
  (2) percent of persons 25+ with less than 9 years of school
  (3) percent of persons 25+ with high school or more
Family Structural block consists of:
  (1) divorces per 1000 adults
  (2) percent of non-married couple families
  (3) percent of families with a female head
  (4) percent of females divorced

out earlier that births to teens could easily be categorized as a socioeconomic family structure, or even public health variable. Its suitability to any of those categories will be justified in later discussion. Since one of the main purposes of this procedure was to differentiate between the capacities of each of the three primary domains to explain variance in maltreatment rates, birth to teens was omitted from this analysis.

Family structural variables accounted for more variance in the rate of reported abuse when entered first than did the other two variable sets--20.76 percent vs. 15.8 percent for economic and 11.8 percent for educational variables. Education exhibited a separate and distinct effect from economic standing. Median home value ($t = 2.86$, $p = .005$) and the percentage of adults who completed less than nine years of formal education ($t = 2.25$, $p = .026$) were the only items singularly significant in the final equation.

Socioeconomic status was more directly linked with child neglect. Income and other indicators of financial position were most important. But the entry of family structural variables substantially augmented the explanatory strength of the data set. Median home value ($t = 2.02$, $p = .046$), median family income ($t = 2.39$, $p = .019$) and the percentage of females divorced ($t = 2.46$, $p = .016$) were significant among the 12 items used in the analysis. While each component of socioeconomic stratum accounted for more variance than the family structure dimension when entered first into the regression equation, their explanatory power was complementary. The association of the 12 variables with rates of reported neglect considerably exceeded that with any other form of maltreatment. Almost half of the variance in child neglect rates was explained.

Less than one-third of the variance in rates of physical abuse was related to the three variable sets. Family structure accounted for about 70 percent of the total association. Even when entered last into the regression equation, the family structure block provided more explanation than the components of socioeconomic status combined.

Sexual abuse was weakest in its relationship to the three blocks of variables. Family structure was somewhat more explanatory than the socioeconomic dimensions. But less than one-fourth of the variance in rates of reported sexual abuse was accounted for. Each variable set contained one variable either significant or approaching significance in the ultimate equation: (1) percentage of females divorced ($t = 3.68$, $p = < .001$), (2) percentage of families below the poverty level ($t = 1.95$, $p = .054$), and (3) percentage of persons 25+ years with less than 9 years of school ($t = 1.97$, $p = .051$).

Discrimination of Risk

Discriminant analysis is a powerful technique for identifying differences between groups. Most of the basic assumptions necessary to discriminant analysis are also required for regression analysis. But the dependent variable explained by the discriminant function may be measured at the nominal level. Many times the researcher is more interested in correctly classifying cases with regard to their value on the dependent variable rather than determining the ways in which groups differ. The classification of counties as either high or low incidence for child maltreatment was the purpose of this discriminant analysis.

The number of cases analyzed must exceed the number of variables used in discriminant analyses by more than two (Klecka, 1980). But that is the only practical constraint on the number of discriminating variables, and when they are numerous this procedure is analogous to the multiple regression technique which has been used previously. As with regression analysis, the independent variables must be interval-level data items. The conditions required for discriminant analysis are not restrictive to most applications which employ the type of information assembled for the purposes of this study.

Sixty counties with a population of more than 100,000 were analyzed. They were the 30 with the lowest rates of reported child maltreatment (fewer than 5.54 per 1000 children) and the 30 counties with the highest rates of reports (more than 11.08 per 1000 children). Each group was comprised of roughly one-quarter (25.6 percent) of all counties with at least 100,000 residents. All counties in the high incidence group had rates at least double that of any county in the low incidence group. Discriminant analysis was employed in an effort to discern this substantial separation between groups through examination of the 33 environmental variables used in the preceding regression analyses.

The problem to be overcome by this procedure is tantamount to the one faced annually by social service administrators attempting equitably to ration precious clinical resources in a manner consistent with some anticipation of the distribution of child maltreatment cases throughout a prescribed service area. The independent variables are used to classify counties by rates of maltreatment. Miscalculation carries with it a high cost. Workers will be seriously overextended in some areas but not others, the situation that currently exists within this country's child protection system. But the likelihood that cases of child mistreatment will be inadequately attended is much more damaging. The inability to differentiate even between regions in which very high versus low prevalences of abuse and neglect should be expected has been detrimental to the credibility of the child protection profession. The lack of fundamental understanding of the etiology of maltreatment which these critical decisions require has eroded confidence within, as well as outside, the system.

Just one discriminant function was derived in the effort to categorize the 60 counties on the basis of their 1980 rates of reported child mistreatment as efficiently as possible. The social, health and economic variables were entered directly into the function. Wilks' Lambda was .3639, indicating the significant discriminating power of the variables used in the analysis. The eigenvalue of 1.7482 and canonical correlation of .798 denote the fact that the function was very powerful in its ability to separate the two groups. Figure 4.1 portrays the practical efficacy of this procedure. The respective group centroids are widely separated by the discriminant scores computed for each case.

Classification was correct for 88.3 percent of the counties, and the error tended to fall on the side of overestimation. That is, 33 counties were assigned to the high risk group. 'Sensitivity' and 'specificity' are concepts important to understanding the value of a procedure in risk assessment. Sensitivity is the index of the ability of a procedure to detect risk when present. Specificity, on the other hand, is a measure of a technique to screen out cases characterized by an absence of risk. Twenty-eight (93.3 percent) of the high incidence counties were correctly identified, while 82.5 percent of low incidence counties were properly classified. There were five false positives, but only two false negatives. It should be of interest to analysts preoccupied with predictive tasks that sensitivity and specificity are considered stable properties (McMaster University Department of Clinical Epidemiology and Biostatistics, 1981) since they are not affected by changing the proportion of analyzed units with high versus low incidence. The careful examination of environmental variables has the potential to preclude some of the most grossly erroneous judgments which can taint legislative and public perception of the expertise of members of the child protection field. For this application, had the normal per capita (constant worker: child ratio) method of personnel allocation been used, child protection personnel serving the 30 counties with the highest rates of maltreatment would have had caseloads much more than twice the size of workers in the counties with the lowest incidence rates. Such events are severely detrimental to the morale of beleaguered child protection personnel.

Intra-State Analysis

The potential sources of variation in inter-state maltreatment rates, speak to the need for intra-state analyses. Table 29 reveals that environmental factors were more efficacious in accounting for rates of child mistreatment when controlling for these state-to-state differences. The table depicts the

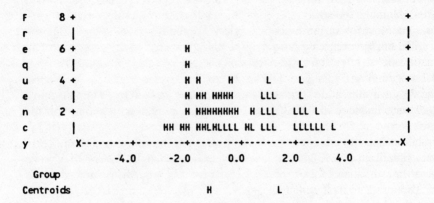

```
F    8 +                                                                      +
r      |                                                                      |
e    6 +                          H                                           +
q      |                          H                      L                    |
u    4 +                          H H      H      L      L                     +
e      |                          H HH HHHH     LLL      L                     |
n    2 +                          H HHHHHHHH  H LLL    LLL L                    +
c      |                       HH HH HHLHLLLL HL LLL     LLLLLL L               |
y         X---------+---------+---------+---------+---------+---------X
                 -4.0      -2.0       0.0       2.0       4.0
  Group
Centroids                         H              L
```

Classification Results -

Actual Group	No. of Cases	Predicted Group Low	Predicted Group High
Low	30	25 83.3%	5 16.7%
High	30	2 6.7%	28 93.3%

Percent of cases correctly classified: 88.33%

Symbols for histogram plot:
  L - County with low rate of child maltreatment (less than 5.54 per 1000)
  H - County with high rate of child maltreatment (greater than 11.08 per 1000)

NOTE: Counties depicted had the most extreme rates of child maltreatment among
        the 117 study counties with a population of at least 100,000.

FIGURE 4.1. Stacked histogram for canonical discriminant function of
classification of counties with high vs. low rates of child maltreatment on the
basis of 33 environmental variables

results for study states with at least 30 counties. Even with inclusion of the analytically troublesome, sparsely populated counties, these state-by-state environmental explanations of abuse and neglect were for the most part more powerful than for the 117 largest counties across the 18 state study area. Notably, the social and economic variables were much more effective in accounting for variance among county rates of sexual abuse.

The multiple regression equation which produced the results for the estimation of rates for reported child maltreatment previously shown in Table 4.7 was employed to analyze interstate variance in the explanatory power of the 33 environmental variables. Counties of the 12 states listed in Table 4.29 were included in the analysis. The difference between the actual rate of reported mistreatment in the county and that estimated by the regression equation constituted the dependent variable. Inter-state differences were very significant $F (11, 862) = 3.43, p < .001$. They ranged from an average error in estimation of 2.50 reported cases per 1000 children for the counties of Minnesota to 4.62 per 1000 children for Indiana counties. It may seem that this increased analytical success obtained by restricting geographically the study focus is not as important as if it had been achieved across states. But the operation of our child protection system is for the most part county based. County personnel resources are dictated by state departments of social services consistent with the intent of state legislatures. The relative child protection need of an Oklahoma county vs. that of a county in the state of Texas will have no effect on the allocation of resources to meet the needs of the two respective areas. But comparison of the needs of one Texas county to those of another does have definite funding implications.

Effect of the Size of the Unit of Analysis

The states of New York and Missouri were used to demonstrate the magnitude and nature of the effect of modestly populated units of analysis. New York had the greatest population of any of the 18 study states, second only to California in 1980, more than 18 million people. With just 62 counties, New York exhibited the highest average county population of any state, and had 25 counties with more than 100,000 inhabitants. Given the relationship of associations between environmental and child maltreatment variables to county population, New York would seem optimally populated and county configured to produce strong ecological correlations.

Missouri stands in stark contrast to New York for the purposes of this analysis. It had the greatest number of counties, 115, but a population in 1980 just in excess of 4 million people. Its average county size was small by comparison with New York. Therefore, in view of the 18-state result, one

TABLE 4.29. Intra-State Correlations Between Child Maltreatment Rates and 33 Environmental Variables for All Counties

State	All Reports		Neglect		Phys Abuse		Sex Abuse	
	r	S.E.	r	S.E.	r	S.E.	r	S.E.
Arkansas	.78*	5.05	.72	8.82	.73	0.95	.72	0.44
Indiana	.61	8.27	.58	5.50	.63	2.24	.64	0.82
Louisiana	.89*	2.36	.87*	4.28	.81	1.63	.68	0.47
Michigan	.90*	3.12	.86*	3.24	N/A	N/A	.81*	0.46
Minnesota	.65	3.17	.60	2.09	.74*	0.41	.73*	0.54
Missouri	.65	4.30	.67*	5.39	.55	0.67	.67*	0.51
Nebraska	.73*	1.61	.62	1.73	.70	0.37	.53	0.29
New Mexico	.96	3.14	.99*	2.17	.97	0.88	.99*	0.14
New York	.82*	1.67	.74	1.68	.78	0.38	.75	0.26
North Dakota	.89	2.82	.84	4.33	.86	0.56	.92*	0.35
South Carolina	.87	1.96	.86	4.11	N/A	N/A	.90*	0.93
Wisconsin	.66	2.71	.68	3.31	.68	1.18	.74	0.59

* p<.05

NOTE: Includes states with at least 30 counties.
      No physical abuse data available for Michigan or South Carolina.

would expect Missouri to yield very modest environmental variables to child maltreatment correlations.

Figures 4.2, 4.3, and 4.4 reflect the results of analysis of these two states. Correlations using all 62 of New York's counties were much greater than found in the examination of all 18 study states. About twice as much of the variance in rates of mistreatment reports was explained within New York (R Squared = .673) vs. within the entire study area. Rates of each form of maltreatment were also accounted for in much larger part by this intra-state analysis (see Table 4.29).

New York affords the analyst the luxury of being able to investigate environmental influence on abuse and neglect in counties with 100,000+ inhabitants within the state. It had 21.4 percent (25 of 117) of the counties with at least this population among the 18 states. Correlations were remarkably high for this subset of counties. The coefficients of correlation indicate the power to virtually predict rates of child mistreatment among these counties. For physical abuse, all but 1.6 percent of the variance in rates between the counties was explained. But the equation employs a large number of variables to examine a relatively small number of cases. As a result, statistical significance was attained for only two of these relationships in spite of the huge values of their correlation coefficients (see Table 4.30).

Missouri with its many sparsely populated counties was characterized by environmental variable to maltreatment rates also superior to those for the 18 state area. While the associations were much weaker than those for New York, due to the greater number of counties (115), all but the relationship for physical abuse either attained or approached statistical significance (see Table 4.29). Clearly, extending the analysis beyond the borders of a single state will result in diminution of the capacity to account for maltreatment rate variance. This observation was further validated by performing the same regression procedures on the counties of the two states combined. Except for child neglect for which associations were virtually the same, correlations were lower for the combination of states than for either of them examined independently of the other. The huge correlations observed for New York were vastly reduced, and even Missouri which represents a sort of worst case scenario for analysis of this type, had recorded associations stronger than for the combination of 177 counties from the two states. These findings reaffirm the futility of small population unit analysis as well as the effect on analyses of expanding the study to areas governed by different bodies with the authority to enact legislation (see Table 4.31). Thus prediction/estimation of incidence for all but heavily populated counties is not encouraged by these findings. Unqualified prediction of rates does not now seem plausible. However, the success observed in estimating rates of child maltreatment for the 25 largest counties of New York State and in discriminating high risk from low risk counties attests to the need for future study of the relationships of environmental variables to child abuse and neglect.

The correlations between rates of child maltreatment and environmental variables have been established. The implications of these findings are discussed in the next chapter.

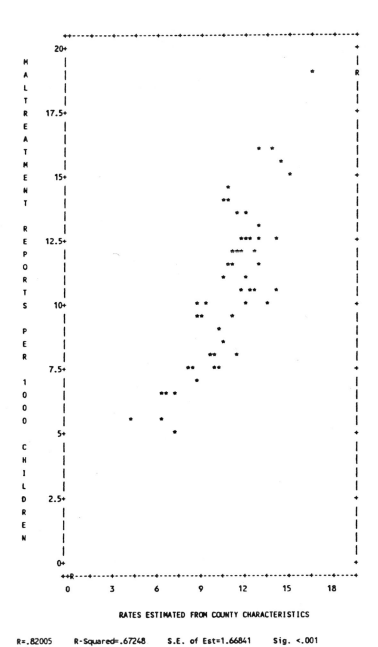

RATES ESTIMATED FROM COUNTY CHARACTERISTICS

R=.82005   R-Squared=.67248   S.E. of Est=1.66841   Sig. <.001

FIGURE 4.2. Actual reports of maltreatment per 1000 children vs. estimated rates based on characteristics of the 62 New York State counties in 1980.

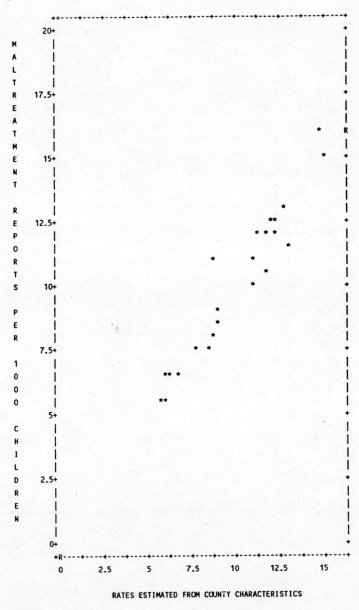

FIGURE 4.3. Actual reports of maltreatment per 1000 children vs. estimated rates based on characteristics of the 25 New York State counties with
more than 100,000 residents in 1980

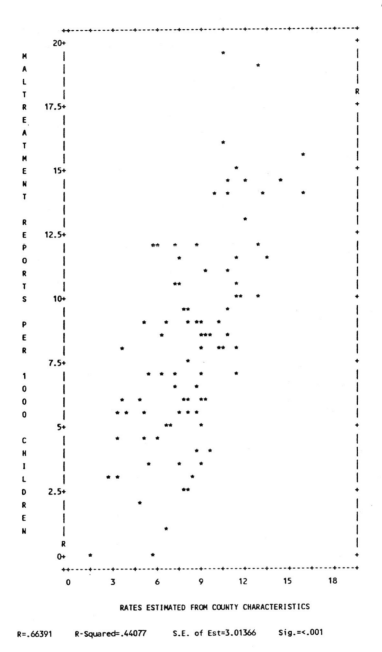

FIGURE 4. 4. Actual reports of maltreatment per 1000 children vs. estimated rates based on characteristics of the 115 Missouri state counties in
1980

TABLE 4.30. Regression of Rates of Reported Child Maltreatment on 33 Environmental Variables for the 25 New York State Counties with More Than 100,000 Residents in 1980

All Maltreatment:
Multiple R	.96
Multiple R Square	.92
Standard Error	1.99

Neglect:
Multiple R	.97
Multiple R Square	.95
Standard Error	.79

Physical Abuse:
Multiple R	.99
Multiple R Square	.98
Standard Error	.11

Sexual Abuse:
Multiple R	.95
Multiple R Square	.90
Standard Error	.11

TABLE 4.31. Regression of Rates of Reported Child Maltreatment on 33 Environmental Variables for the 177 Counties of the States of Missouri and New York in 1980

All Maltreatment:
Multiple R	.64
Multiple R Square	.41
Standard Error	3.61

Neglect:
Multiple R	.68
Multiple R Square	.46
Standard Error	4.35

Physical Abuse:
Multiple R	.52
Multiple R Square	.27
Standard Error	.56

Sexual Abuse:
Multiple R	.60
Multiple R Square	.35
Standard Error	.43

5

Discussion of Study Results

Environmental variables chosen on the basis of the review of literature proved useful in accounting for variance in rates of abuse and neglect. Two were especially strongly correlated with physical abuse and neglect respectively and warrant additional consideration.

Family Structure and the Ability to Provide

The correlations of economic status, education and family structure with rates of child maltreatment were discussed in the previous chapter. The relationship of education with financial position is well known. Parents typically exhort their children that academic achievement is the price for later economic reward. But family structure is also related to financial status. In particular, divorce imposes acute economic hardship on the woman who retains custody of the children born during a previous marriage. She must endure the everyday strain of nurturing her children and providing financially for their needs, usually with very little support. Often alone, the single mother entertains the demands of children whom she may view as a liability to her prospect for remarriage. Abuse and neglect are more common to this family setting than to any other.

The upward surge in divorce rates which occurred during the decades of the 1960's and 1970's precipitated a rate of growth in families headed by a female with children ten times greater than the growth rate of two-parent families (DHHS, 1980). In 1979, for the fourth consecutive year, the average number of children involved in each divorce was 1.0 (U.S. Bureau of the Census). Thus, children are not being spared this emotional experience. They are almost always left dependent primarily upon their mother, although her earning power is usually modest when compared with that of the former male spouse. In 1980, 13.7 percent of all Americans, but 18.6 percent of those younger than 18 years of age, resided in female-headed households. Just 1.2 percent of this country's children lived with a single male head of household in that decennial census year. Only 11.3 percent of children in the

United States were members of households headed by unmarried women in 1970 (U.S. Bureau of the Census, 1981).

In 1979, the median annual income for the two-adult family with children was about three times as great as that for families headed by single women with children ($18,646 vs. $6,502). The poverty rate for families maintained by women with no husband present was 31.9 percent compared with 6.9 percent for all other families. Almost half (48.6 percent) of the children in families headed by a female with no husband present lived in poverty vs. 8.5 percent in other families (DHHS, 1980).

One of the most important aspects of the etiology of child maltreatment would appear to be straightforward. Child maltreatment, especially neglect, epitomizes social phenomena with which ecologists have been concerned, those "which are rooted in the dependence of men on limited supplies of the necessary means to satisfy their needs" (Timasheff, 1967, p. 213). The 'ability to provide' is treated in the AHA definition of child neglect as a dichotomous concept rather than one of degree. A family earning $10,000 per year may be marginally able to provide for most of the basic needs of its children. But a family with $100,000 annual revenue is much better able to do so, and will be required to make few if any sacrifices in fulfilling its fundamental responsibilities to its children. The provision parents make to meet their children's needs relates directly and strongly to the means at their disposal, their capacity to provide for fulfillment of the needs of their children. If this be the case, there can be no quick therapeutic fix to the problem.

The Influence of Adolescent Pregnancy

Teenage pregnancy was sufficiently dominant as a correlate of maltreatment to warrant additional consideration of that phenomenon. Twenty-two percent of all women who gave birth in 1985 were unmarried; this included 51 percent of 18 and 19 year olds and 72 percent of women under the age of 18 (DHHS, 1987). Although they lack the much-needed support which a spouse could provide, an overwhelming majority of teen-age mothers elect to keep and attempt to raise their children (NICHD, 1984). Fewer babies are being offered for adoptive placement (Baldwin, 1983), even though out-of-wedlock births to teen mothers have increased.

Adolescent mothers come poorly prepared to the tasks of parenthood. McAnarney and Aten (1981) noted that the youngest teen mothers are aloof and indifferent while older adolescents tended to be aggressive toward their children. Epstein (1980) observed that very young teens did not improve their caregiving practices even as they acquired parenting experience. Their experience also did little to reduce resentment they harbored for their children. Most of their children are the products of pregnancies that the teen mother neither wanted nor planned (Zelnik & Kantner, 1978). However, her bitterness about having given birth at such a young age simply increases during the first two years of motherhood (Presser, 1974), perhaps as the realization of lost opportunities sets in.

Clearly, the seeds of abuse and neglect are present in this scenario. Studies have shown that child maltreatment is more likely to be inflicted upon children born to an unmarried adolescent mother than to an older married woman (Kinard & Klerman, 1980; Lynch & Roberts, 1977; Sills, Thomas, & Rosenbloom, 1977; Smith, Hanson, & Noble, 1974). In addition, there is the possibility that conception may be the result of sexual abuse. Incestuous relations are a common form of sexual abuse which, should the adolescent victim become impregnated, make the link between child maltreatment and teen pregnancy a direct one. Teen pregnancy spans the environmental variables used in this study more completely than does any of the other items.

The economic disadvantage of adolescent motherhood is a lasting one (McCarthy & Radish, 1983) and virtually assures that both mother and child will depend upon public assistance for their livelihood (NICHD, 1984; Alan Guttmacher Institute, 1981). These women seldom pursue their education even after the baby has been born (Card & Wise, 1978) and are much less likely ever to graduate from high school than women similar to them in personal attributes including previous record of academic achievement (Alan Guttmacher Institute, 1981).

Due to this educational deficit and their parental responsibilities, these young mothers have little earning power and are more often unemployed than women who defer motherhood (Simkins, 1984). The Guttmacher Institute (1981) found that about two-thirds of all families with a female younger than 25 years old heading the household with children of less than preschool age were impoverished, five times the percentage of all families with young children living below the poverty level. Yet, marriage is not a panacea for the financial difficulties of these unfortunate women and their children. Rates of divorce and separation are much greater for them than for married couples in the adult population on first and later marriages (NICHD, 1984; Sklar & Berkov, 1974).

Teen pregnancy also departed from the pattern of most other independent variables which were associated with just certain forms of child maltreatment and usually only for counties of one or two of the population categories. Births to teens correlated significantly with all child maltreatment reports and each particular form of mistreatment for all population county groups with one exception. Only two variables correlated statistically significantly with child sexual abuse for counties with 50,000-99,999 inhabitants. Births to teens approached (p = .063) but did not reach significance. Just 35 percent of the variance was explained by the environmental factors in aggregate for the rates of sexual abuse at that population level.

Forms of Child Maltreatment

The three most prevalent forms of child maltreatment were correlated with one another. The correlation coefficient for the relationship of the incidences of physical abuse to neglect was .69, for physical abuse to sexual abuse was .63 and for neglect to sexual abuse was just .36. Thus, no form shared as much as half of its variance with either of the other two types of child mistreatment. Yet, the various forms of child maltreatment are often grouped indiscriminately.

The results of this study send a mixed message to future prognosticators of maltreatment rates. On one hand, the association of social stressors was stronger with neglect than with any other form of maltreatment. Neglect is presently the most prevalent type of maltreatment, which is definitively linked with socioeconomic factors. Neglect represents the parent's 'failure' to provide for the child. Many of the economic variables examined indicate parental 'inability' to provide. A lack of economic means rather than a lack of interest in the welfare of the child underlies at least some of the widespread incidence of parental neglect.

But social stressor variables were weakest in their explanation of sexual abuse. A sharp increase has been observed in recent years in the percent of total maltreatment which comprises sexual abuse. Unless understanding of its etiology can be enhanced, our capacity to anticipate geographic demand for child protection services will suffer. The relationship of sexual abuse to the other two most prevalent forms of child maltreatment is weak and its pattern of incidence is poorly understood.

Child Protection Laws,
Interstate Variance

Child maltreatment has been federally defined in Public Law 93-237, the Child Abuse Prevention and Treatment Act of 1974:

The physical or mental injury, sexual abuse, negligent treatment, or maltreatment of a child under the age of eighteen by a person who is responsible for the child's welfare under circumstances which would indicate that the child's health or welfare is harmed or threatened thereby.

But as Gelles (1987) has pointed out, each state has promulgated its own law defining the abuse and neglect of children. Litigation has been initiated by the state to prosecute child abusers and by individuals accused of perpetrating child maltreatment to have their records of alleged abuse or neglect stricken from state central registries. About one-third of the requests of alleged perpetrators to have their names expunged from the Colorado Child Abuse and Neglect Central Registry in 1985 were granted by a fair hearing officer or district court (Colorado Department of Social Services, 1986). The decisions handed down by the court have greatly influenced the operational definition of child maltreatment. The matter is no longer as simple as Kempe's clinical decision in the early 1960's to award a medical diagnosis to an injury intentionally inflicted by the child's caretaker. But most of the prerogative to legislate and interpret now clearly belongs to the states. And while county agencies conduct field operations required to protect children in accordance with existing state law, state departments of social service allocate personnel and other resources for that purpose consistent with legislative intent. State departments of social service also maintain the official central registry containing records of child maltreatment and the identity of perpetrators.

While there is state-to-state variation in the statutory definition of child child maltreatment (Education Commission of the States, 1979), Myers and Peters (1987, p. 27) contend that:

It is possible, however, to distill common themes from the various definitions. Physical abuse consists of non-accidental physical injury or trauma. The statutes of most states provide a separate definition for sexual abuse. Many statutes define sexual abuse as any sexual contact or activity that is prohibited by criminal law. The reporting laws require reporting of neglect as well as abuse. Neglect is a protean concept embracing such matters as parental failure to provide basic necessities such as food, clothing, shelter, and medical care. In many states, neglect includes inadequate parenting.

Although Myers and Peters (1987) have noted some general commonality among state legal definitions of the forms of child maltreatment, their comprehensive presentation of state child protection statutes suggests that differences in the form and content of those statutes may account for some of the interstate variance observed in rates of child abuse and neglect. No single comparison among states is sufficient as a basis for general inference, but an intra-regional comparison of the legal definition of child sexual abuse exemplifies differences in state laws. The exhaustive description of the act which constitutes child sexual assault in the state of Texas has been extracted from Texas Penal Code Annotated, Section 22.011:

(a) A person commits an offense if the person:
   (1) intentionally or knowingly
      (A) causes the penetration of the anus or female sexual organ of another person who is not the spouse of actor by any means, without that person's consent, or contact actor, without that person's consent; or
      (B) causes the penetration of the mouth of another person who is not the spouse of the actor, without that person's consent, or contact actor, without that person's consent; or
      (C) causes the sexual organ of another person who is not the spouse of the actor, without that person's consent, to contact, or penetrate the mouth, anus, or sexual organ of another person, including the actor; or
   (2) intentionally or knowingly:
      (A) causes the penetration of the anus or female sexual organ of a child by any means;
      (B) causes the penetration of the mouth of a child by the sexual organ of the actor; or
      (C) causes the sexual organ of a child to contact or penetrate the mouth, anus, or sexual organ of another person, including the actor.
(b) A sexual assault under Subsection (a)(1) of this section is without the consent of the other person if:
   (1) the actor compels the other person to submit or participate by the use of the use of physical force or violence;
   (2) the actor compels the other person to submit or participate by threatening to use force or violence against the other person, and the other person believes that the actor has the present ability to execute the threat;
   (3) the other person has not consented and the actor knows the other person is unconscious or physically unable to resist;
   (4) the actor knows that as a result of mental disease or defect the other person is at the time of the sexual assault incapable either of appraising the nature of the act or of resisting it;
   (5) the other person has not consented and the actor knows the other person is unaware that the sexual assault is occurring;
   (6) the actor knows that the other person submits or participates because of the erroneous belief that the actor is the other person's spouse;
   (7) the actor has intentionally impaired the person's power to appraise or control the other person's conduct by administering any substance without the other person's knowledge; or

(8)   the actor compels the other person to submit or participate by threatening to use force or violence against any person, and the other person believes that the actor has the ability to execute the threat.

(c) In this section:

(1)   "Child" means a person younger than 17 years of age who is not the spouse of the actor.

That part of the legal code of an adjacent state, Louisiana, that has been devoted to sexual assault stands in sharp contrast to Texas' explicit treatment of the offense. Discussion of child sexual abuse has been tersely embedded along with other forms of abuse in a single paragraph of Louisiana Civil Code Annotated, Article 14, p. 403:

(3) "Abuse" is the infliction, by a person responsible for the child's care, of physical or mental injury of the causing of the deterioration of a child including but not limited to such means as sexual abuse, sexual exploitation, or the exploitation or overwork of a child to such an extent that his health or moral or emotional well-being is endangered. (p. 403)

Court decisions concerning sexual abuse cases in these two states may in practice not reflect these differences in form and content of the applicable legal code. But certainly the variations do allow for possible discrepant treatment of the same case if tried in each of the two respective states.

Other features of child protection laws appear to be related to rates of reported mistreatment. Half of the 18 states and 27 of all 51 require that reports of child abuse and neglect be made to law enforcement officials as well as to departments of social service. There has been considerable debate concerning the implications of police involvement in child mistreatment cases. Abusive parents sometimes see no compelling reason to comply with the treatment plans of child protection personnel. Thus, the authority implicit in enforcement of the law can be viewed as a necessity in many cases. All but seven states now have provision for criminal penalties in their legal statutes. Opponents of a law enforcement role perceive contradiction in filing accusations with an agency possessing criminal investigatory authority and simultaneously attempting to provide human services. They argue that treatment and law enforcement are incompatible activities. The situation which evolves discourages candor in worker-abusive parent communication as the client becomes apprehensive that full disclosure of wrong-doing may result in criminal prosecution. Rates of reported maltreatment in states that require police notification are lower than in states without this requirement.

The former had a combined rate of 7.58 reports per 1000 children (79,434 reports and 10,482,287 residents younger than 18 years of age) vs. 9.49 per 1000 children (80,661 reports and 8,495,917 resident children) for states requiring just social service department notification. This suggests that abusive adults and/or professionals mandated to report are inhibited from disclosure of child maltreatment by possible police involvement. State child abuse and neglect laws abrogate the protection of otherwise privileged communications between certain types of professionals and their patients or clients. Virtually all other information exchanged between a physician and his/her patients can be excluded from evidence in a judicial proceeding. But that which pertains to child maltreatment is not exempted from court proceedings in most states. No state has abrogated the attorney-client privilege because of the importance of confidential exchange in the preparation of a defense in cases of criminal prosecution. But 13 states, 6 of which were among the 18 study states, have revoked the protection of privileged communication between individuals and all other professionals in cases of suspected or known child mistreatment. This includes communication with mental health therapists, the clergy, and physicians of all medical specialties. These 6 states exhibited greater rates than did the other 12 studied, 9.78 vs. 7.81 reports per 1000 children (58,796 for 6,011,172 resident children vs. 101,299 for 12,967,032 children). The requirement for professionals to report information once kept in strict confidence does seem to influence the reporting rate. Thus, states similar in social and economic characteristics can differ in child maltreatment rates due to differences in their legal and child protection systems, as well as the variety of other items not included in this analysis.

6

Recommendations

The products of this extensive analysis of the etiology of child maltreatment suggest a useful agenda for activities in the field.

Refocusing Service: A Comprehensive Stress Model

While Americans' inaccessibility to medical care is due to geographic and specialty maldistribution, the difficulty in the child protection field is attributable to both geographic maldistribution and an actual shortage of trained professionals. But systematically derived indices of need for medical service are applied uniformly throughout the country to address physician shortages. One such index, the Medical Underservice Index (MUI), is an additive scale of weighted scores for the infant mortality rate, the percentage of the population below the poverty level, the percentage of the population 65 years of age or older, and the primary care physician to population ratio. No such comprehensive indicator of the need for child protection personnel has been formulated. Yet, the variables assembled here to explain variance in reports of maltreatment were extracted from the Area Resource File used by its sponsor, the Bureau of Health Professions, to designate primary care health manpower shortage areas and medically underserved areas. This fact begs the question, "Why have such empirical measures of need for child protection workers not yet been developed?" The problem of configuring the child protection system regionally does seem similar to the task of matching the delivery of medical care to the needs of communities and counties.

The interaction of stimulus and response is now viewed as the complete representation of stress (Pearlin et al., 1981; Pearlin & Aneshensel, 1986). As such, the full concept of stress consists of a complex process rather than a life event or individual characteristic.

Epidemiologists recognize that both stimulus and response are indispensable to a sequential screen in their studies of disease conditions

(Pearlin & Aneshensel, 1986). Given the level of environmental stressors, a certain resistance on the part of the individual is required to prevent maladaptive behavior which is then seen as a manifestation of stress. The role of social stressors in precipitating the mistreatment of children has comprised the content of this study. However, the stress equation from a broad perspective also consists of human reactions to environmental conditions and experiences which constitute stressors. Stress signifies an imbalance between the response capability of an individual and the demands that are placed upon him (McGrath, 1970).

Child maltreatment and other violent behaviors may be emitted when the individual's adaptive resources are overwhelmed by the demands with which they are challenged. The inability to contend with social pressures with which individuals are confronted is of course implied in the observation of child maltreatment; evidence of 'a substantial imbalance' between stress and the capacity to resist it. The variables found to be associated with child maltreatment, such as income and education clearly qualify as 'social stressors'--sources of the human behavior that clinicians interpret as a manifestation of stress.

Clearly, the environmental pressures associated with a high incidence of child maltreatment are also related to the prevalence of other forms of deviance (Gil, 1979). Substance abuse has been determined to be prevalent in abusive families (Baily & Baily, 1985; Bennett & Pethybridge, 1979; Fitch & Papantonio, 1983; Mayer & Black, 1977; National Indian Child Abuse and Neglect Resource Center, 1980; Steinmetz, 1980; Wethers, 1978). Researchers have observed many of the socioeconomic stressors--poverty or insufficient income, and unemployment--known to correlate with child abuse and neglect, in maltreating families in which substance abuse was taking place (Baily & Baily, 1985; Bennett & Pethybridge, 1979; Fitch & Papantonio, 1983; Mayer & Black, 1977; National Indian Child Abuse and Neglect Resource Center, 1980; Steinmetz, 1980).

This has prompted some researchers to regard child abuse as a symptom of underlying stress in the same way that crime or substance abuse might be regarded (Pavenstedt & Bernard, 1971). It suggests that child maltreatment may be part of a much larger constellation of deviant behavior. Factors which provide a 'triggering context' for child abuse or neglect for one parent can precipitate substance abuse for another. Or, as some research indicates, these stresses can lead to both forms of deviant behavior. Child abuse can therefore be seen along with other deviant acts, as a part of the symptomatology of family distress that can be traced to external circumstances (van Rees, 1978) and as a reflection of the inability of the family to withstand the many stresses created by our changing society (Savells & Bash, 1979).

Because of clinical belief in the linkage of stress and abusive and neglectful parental behavior, new programs seek to protect children by reducing stress experienced by their parents. That objective has usually been addressed by the provision of respite care (Subramanian, 1985; Weltz, 1984) in which a temporary home for is provided for children whose parents are unable to cope during a period of extreme stress. Parents may then be treated to elevate their diminished capacity to master stressful forces. But the psychological state of the family upon which most therapists focus almost exclusively, is contingent upon environmental factors (Cappell & Mays, 1973). The combination of strong external sources of stress and a very limited range of response alternatives is the condition posing the most danger to the child from parental abuse.

Unfortunately, interventions currently available to abusive families do not deal with one of the two major components of the stress equation. More comprehensive programs directed toward social stressors--the actual sources of the stress--are desperately needed.

Large-Scale Ecological Study

The ecological method is not new to the study of social problems. It was made popular by what has been termed the Chicago School, the University of Chicago's influential department of sociology. The work of Park and Burgess was paramount in advancing early ecological study, much of which focused on urban life (Vine, 1969). They, in fact, used Chicago as their ecological laboratory and encouraged their students to do likewise.

Ecologists have utilized social class and geographic location in studies of the incidence of mental disorder. The social stratum of schizophrenics at the time they are diagnosed and the characteristics of their community have drawn special attention (Freedman, Kaplan & Sadock, 1972).

Thus, the ecological method has a tradition of service to the social sciences, particularly in the study of mental health. Its past record of utility in examining the incidence of deviant behavior across geographic units suggested the suitability of its application in future investigation of the etiology of child maltreatment.

Ecologists have been faulted for being excessively zealous in the interpretation of their results and overemphasizing the role of deteriorated local habitat in their explanations of social phenomena (Timasheff, 1967):

One often has the impression that, in the authors' minds, the very walls and roofs of the dilapidated buildings and the unsightly dirt of the streets themselves shape behavior. (p. 214)

There are certainly hazards related to the interpretation of ecological correlations in the absence of data for which the individual is the unit of analysis. The practical limitations of this method have long been known (Faris, 1944; Dunham, 1947; Robinson, 1950). Last (1983) has defined the dreaded condition for which correlations found in the course of examination of population units do not pertain to indi- viduals who are members of those units:

> An error in inference due to failure to distinguish between different levels of organization. A correlation between variables based on group (ecological) characteristics is not necessarily reproduced between variables based on individual characteristics; an association at one level may disappear at another, or even be reversed. (p. 31)

The problem occurs, therefore, when inferences are made to units other than the ones analyzed (Nachmias & Nachmias, 1981). Durkheim (1897, 1951) has been cited for this methodological violation in his analysis of suicide (Selvin, 1965).

Theorists who have disregarded the possible distortion associated with generalization to smaller population units have in fact disserved their method and the audience for their arguments. But these procedures are most useful when employed to identify and describe the environs in which the problem may be most likely to occur. When studies of social phenomena consist of both traditional ecological correlations and the analysis of data applicable to individuals or subsets of the population units ecologically examined, as in this analysis, the usually troublesome assumptions inherent in the ecological method can be validated. Also it has been demonstrated that when the unit of actual interest is a group or geographic unit rather than individuals, ecological associations are particularly needed (Menzel, 1950). Thus, a state department of social services administrator allocating resources to county child protection agencies may be better informed by the results of an ecological analysis than a social scientist who is preoccupied with the specific factors which lead to abuse and neglect.

Data obtained from the American Humane Association for use in this study of correlates of child maltreatment were extracted from the individual records of reported cases of child abuse and neglect. The structure of the family of the victimized child, his/her relationship to the perpetrator, was available for individual cases. Public assistance status, race, and stress factors were known for abusive and neglectful families. Had Durkheim been privileged to the same information on individuals who committed suicide, Selvin (1965) concedes that some of the criticism that has been directed toward his method could have been avoided. Similarly, Clausen and Kohn (1954) allow that the relationships postulated between mental illness and environmental variables would have been defensible if they had been founded on information pertaining to individuals, as well as geographic units.

Clausen and Kohn (1954) have remarked that ecological analyses usually leave investigators stranded in mid-stream. But the analyst in the middle of the stream need not be stranded. There is frequently the prospect for continued study of social phenomena employing non-ecological means to build upon knowledge gained through ecological correlation. Ecological investigation is often founded on secondary analysis of existing data. As Rose (1972) has noted, decision makers support analytical processes only when the utility of their findings promises to exceed the cost of conducting them. For this reason, reliance on the use of secondary data has become commonplace.

The Denver Research Institute (1974) has discussed the advantages vs. disadvantages of assessing need without the collection of primary data. Because the secondary data exist prior to design of the research, analysts must make do with the examination of items which may not fully operationalize concepts critical to the study. Survey research is frequently viewed as prohibitively expensive, especially when done nationwide as would have been required by the present study. However, once a social problem has undergone ecological scrutiny, primary data collection may be required to resolve issues still outstanding.

Exploring Relationships Among
Rival Etiological Theories

Debate continues in the child protection field concerning the existence of an intergenerational cycle of child maltreatment. The persistence of child mistreatment from one family generation to the next is not a matter which will be addressed as part of our decennial national census. Clinical investigators have provided virtually all of the support for the intergenerational cycle precisely because of their advantaged position of direct contact with victims and perpetrators.

Sociological theories which have been represented as antithetical to psychodynamic theory have been advanced chiefly by a discipline that has no clinical component, and therefore honors the results of empirical research much more than clinical impression. This is certainly not to say that one discipline is more developed methodologically than another. Rather, it is simply to note that sociologists do not have the opportunity for direct observation available to many psychologists, physicians and social workers. Thus, it is not surprising that most sociological researchers and theorists are not completely taken with the clinical documentation for the existence of an intergenerational cycle of abuse. Yet there is a small body of empirical evidence for the psychodynamic theory of child maltreatment which suggests that it may share common ground with theories which emphasize the importance of environmental factors.

Perhaps the strongest indication that sociological and psychodynamic theories are not diametrically opposed, nor mutually exclusive, was provided by Gelles (1985). From the same representative national survey of 2,143 American families, from which Gelles gained insight into the importance of environmental forces in the causation of child maltreatment, came powerful evidence that adults abused as children tended to exhibit violence toward other family members. Two huge data collection projects in the province of Quebec, Canada, one before and one after implementation of child protection legislation, disclosed that perpetrating parents frequently had a history of victimization as children (Quebec Ministry of Justice, 1984).

A random subsample of 45 abusive families was drawn from AFDC recipients in New Jersey (Horowitz & Wolock, 1981). Twenty-nine percent of the maltreating caretakers had survived severe physical abuse as children. Jameson and Schellenbach (1977) examined the attributes and case histories of 82 perpetrators of child abuse. A disproportionately high percentage of abusive women, but not men, had been mistreated as a child.

These studies do not exhaust the empirical evidence of an intergenerational cycle of abuse, but each is important for a quality besides its support for the psychodynamic theory. Every one of these studies also produced strong documentation of the influence of environmental factors on the incidence of child mistreatment. This raises the question of whether proof of one theory is necessarily refutation of the other. Indeed, is there any reason to believe that sociological and psychological forces can't act in concert? How might their influences perpetuate one another?

In four large-scale studies these theories did not contradict. Patient histories that are collected by treating clinicians typically indicate whether or not the perpetrators of maltreatment were themselves victims of abuse or neglect during childhood, as well as the economic and demographic charac-teristics of the abusive families participating in therapy. This information is generally reported for study samples along with research methods and results. Linking these items with the sociodemographic attributes of the perpetrator's family during his/her youth would indicate if both abusive generations were subjected to many of the same social and economic forces found by this study to be associated with child maltreatment. Because downward mobility is rare in our society (Blau & Duncan, 1964; Featherman & Hauser, 1978), the environmental forces at work on the socioeconomically disadvantaged perpetrator must be similar to, or the same as, some of those to which the parents were earlier subjected. The victims of past abuse who were raised, and now live, in poverty would substantiate both theories by abusing or neglecting their own children.

While cogent arguments for both perspectives have been put forward, the preponderance of scientific evidence does seem more supportive of the socio-logical formulation of child mistreatment. Sociodemographic data are available for the residents of this country or virtually any of its geopolitical units for needs assessment purposes. In this regard, sociologists do not stand at a disadvantage to clinicians or the scholars of other disciplines in their efforts to devise models predictive of human need. The conduct of elaborate psychosocial tests or prolonged clinical observation of the general population is of course not feasible. Yet, clinical data, at least pertaining to perpetrators' past history of victimization, are now needed to validate the possible compatibility between these two perspectives.

Increasing the Suitability of Public Data Sets
for Comparative Analyses

In any secondary analysis of existing data, there is information not available in the data set which could have strengthened the arguments put forward and shed additional light on the subject matter. However, the linkage in this study of just two important data sets, the American Humane Association's National Study File and the Area Resource File, has enabled examination of relationships among environmental and child maltreatment variables on a larger scale than ever undertaken previously. Yet, the vast range of data used in characterizing the generalpopulation of the 18 state area studied were for the most part products of the last national decennial census. Comprehensive periodic updating of this material would be an awesome task. Intercensal adjustment is not currently plausible, particularly since the quinquennial census once contemplated by the U.S. Bureau of the Census was not conducted.

As we have now begun a new decade, it is incumbent upon us to assess the adequacy of provision made to employ 1990 census data in serious, timely study of the problems of our society. The social forces which fuel child maltreatment change in nature and intensity, and attention must now be given to the collection of data appropriate to their measurement.

One aspect of earlier research which was found to facilitate the explanation of rates of child mistreatment is the aggregation of reports over time (Fryer, 1990). Rates predicated on five years of abuse and neglect reporting are more stable than those founded on a single year's reports. Aggregation of this sort negates some of the effect of the small number problems often encountered in the study of remote rural areas. But these procedures bring with them their own set of problems. Most of the difficulty relates to interpretation of their products. With a phenomenon such as child abuse, which has exhibited rapid annual growth in its rate of incidence, do the changes during the study period render some measure of central tendency for that entire period meaningless? The annualized average for maltreatment rates during any five-year period studied since the institution of mandatory reporting will almost without exception be substantially greater than for the first year of the study period, and less than for the final year. In addition, legislators have not paid attention to data which were compiled over a duration of time greater than their own terms of office.

One option is to assemble information for analysis on larger geographic units. The reasons for a county orientation in this analysis have been fully explained. But considerations related to the actual application of study findings aside, there are technical barriers to the aggregation of counties into larger geographic units for examination. Some states do have some version of planning and management regions, but the criteria for regional assignment varies markedly between states. There is no prominent census unit below the state level into which counties are grouped. State economic areas (SEA's) are counties or groups of counties similar in social and economic characteristics, and bounded in such a way that they differ significantly from adjoining areas (U.S. Census Bureau, 1983). But these areas have not been reviewed for the appropriateness of their delineation since the 1970 national census. The 'county group' consists of contiguous counties that have been assembled into logical analytical units for the purposes of persons and organizations using public-use microdata samples, a product of the U.S. Census Bureau. However, these groupings sometimes cross state lines, restricting severely the number of applications for which they are suitable. Therefore, a serious impediment clearly exists to the systematic study of county combinations. A meaningful census designated unit is needed to fill this void.

The results of the 1990 national census will afford a valuable opportunity to examine the sensitivity of the respective forms of child mistreatment to changes in the environmental variables with which they were found to be associated. Intercensal data are not adequate to support detailed broad reexamination of these relationships. If they have endured, increases and declines in rates of reported abuse and neglect should be reflected in corresponding social and economic change. The most valuable variable relationships which can be employed in the construction of social theories are those which will withstand the test of time.

Conclusions from reexamination of these same relationships for subsequent years must be drawn with care. The results of future analyses could contradict the findings of this study for reasons which offer an additional challenge to human service professionals. Critics of the treatment component of the child protection system have implied that failure to address authentic etiological factors deeply embedded in the environment stem from the public's desire to avoid the huge cost of major reconfiguration of social and economic arrangements. The elimination of poverty will be expensive. Yet, those who have been critical have ignored the possibility that large investments from the public tax base which remove certain of the correlates of child maltreatment might not serve to reduce the incidence of abuse and neglect. If poverty is strongly related to the parental mistreatment of children, will its removal coincide with a reduction in rates of child abuse and neglect? This question has not been answered. Lieberson (1985) has described the dilemma posed by asymmetry in relationships among variables. With symmetrical associations:

> The influence of a particular value of X on Y will not be altered by the direction of the change in X. In other words, the movement of X from 15 to 20 may have a different influence on Y than an increase from 5 to 10, but in either case, the movement of X back from 20 to 15 or from 10 to 5 will return Y to its starting point as well. (p. 64)

Relationships among variables are often irreversible. Reduction in the strength of a correlate of child mistreatment may very well not precipitate a decline in rates of abuse. Regrettably, there are no assurances with either of the two principal approaches to child protection. In spite of this important caveat, it is imperative that use be made of public data sets to measure the effect of changes in policies, programs and practices intended to reduce child maltreatment and its effects. There is no substitute for well-designed longitudinal analyses for these purposes. Such analyses can meaningfully inform child protection case management and policy formulation.

7

Conclusion

Definitive restatement of recommendations based on this study are in order. Underlying each is improved understanding of the power of social forces on the members of abusive and neglectful families.

(1) Use environmental data to assess the relative risk of maltreatment of children in specified geographic regions. Secondary data is available for this purpose and has been shown to be useful in this study. Intelligent applicationss of the results of these analyses can significantly improve the allocation of resources on a per capita basis, as illustrated by the preceding discriminate analysis.

But mere conduct of an analysis is not enough. There must be a commitment to action indicated necessary by the results of any such assessment. The earlier described process for designating medically underserved areas for health care is not a 'hollow' one. On the basis of those designations, the Federal government funds community health centers, national health service corps personnel placements, etc. Only when the allocation of child protection resources is linked to their outcome will these objective, empirical efforts have impact.

(2) Adopt a more comprehensive perspective in evaluating the clinical needs of abusive parents, one which takes into account environmental forces to which perpetrators are subjected. This is intuitively unappealing to clinicians. Almost all employ treatment models which embrace psychological principles of accepted behavior. To be sure, individuals possess varying capacities to cope with 'social stressors.' But whatever their predisposition, their strength to withstand, social conditions are a determinant of their behavior. Surely, abusive parents hardened by lifetimes of poverty are disillusioned by a therapist's disregard of their impoverished background. Given the high proportion of perpetrators who are socioeconomically disadvantaged, failure to appreciate the social context in which they mistreat children is especially damaging to treatment efficacy.

(3) Examine the relationship between environmental and intergenerational cycle theories of the etiology of child abuse and neglect. Evidence presented in the preceding chapter suggests that they may in fact be compatible theories which are most valuable when used in tandem. However, the battle lines between the two theoretical camps have long been drawn. The rhetoric exchanged has not always been constructive and interdisciplinary collabo-

ration is needed. Primary data collection of a type that can only be done in a clinician's office, if it is to be unobtrusive, will be required. Yet, the skills of scholars inclined to analyze huge public data sets are also necessary. Cooperation of this sort has been achieved in the study of other phenomena. It is particularly needed in this field. Some meaningful synthesis may be attainable.

(4) Increase the provisions of public data sets to facilitate important analyses of the nature, prevalence and consequences of child maltreatment and the effectiveness of efforts to protect children. Human service professionals must articulate their needs to agencies with a public mandate to collect data: U.S. Bureau of the Census, National Center for Health Statistics, etc. Historically, this has not been well done, and seldom thoughtfully attempted. This task primarily entails specifying items of data and making convincing arguments of need for their collection. It is not the place of representatives of the data collection agency to anticipate the many needs of service provider agencies or to make judgments in isolation concerning their relative importance.

There is much yet to be done. There was more unexplained than explained variance in rates of all reported maltreatment and sexual abuse. This is disturbing since no less than 33 variables were assembled to account for the variation in rates, and those items are only available for such widespread geographic application once each decade. The three major variable domains (economic, educational, and family structural), which consisted of 12 variables when births to teens was not included, did not approach the explanatory power of the entire regression equation of 33 independent variables. Thus, a large number of variables examined in aggregate are required to describe the relationships between the environment and abuse and neglect. Even then, these associations were only verified for large population units.

Any claim that insights gained from the results of this study will serve the purposes of child protection professionals must be tempered by an awareness that these findings explain only in retrospect. Prediction implies the explanation of future events. This analysis provided perspective concerning what had already taken place. The practical value of this type of information is modest in comparison with that which would prepare the child protection system to meet future service needs. These regression and discriminant analyses are helpful to field operations only inasmuch as they direct attention to actions which will enhance resource allocation and worker responsiveness to the real problems and comprehensive needs of abusive families. To the extent that they merely provide additional commentary on the activities of an already overly scrutinized field of dedicated professionals, these findings will not be welcomed. However, a child protection system which takes into account the impact of the environment on the perpetrators and victims of child maltreatment can better fulfill its crucial social mandate.

Each primary actor in this painful scenario is a victim. Child protection workers are asked to achieve the impossible, to perform duties shorthandedly in accordance with the laws promulgated by state legislators whose appropriation of funds for enforcement is woefully inadequate. The poor are expected to allocate scarce family resources and parent their young as if they were not financially constrained. Unmarried women are given no respite from the strain associated with their sole responsibility both for nurturing and providing economically for their children. Saddest of all is the child who suffers the consequences of these unrealistic expectations of workers with their mandate to protect him and of his parents with their responsibility to attend to his physiological and psychosocial development. None of what has been learned from the results of this analysis in any way justifies the maltreatment of children. It does, however, enable us to better understand why it sometimes occurs.

The media and the American public have been unsparing in their criticism of this country's child protection system. But the prevalence of child maltreatment is after all an indictment of society. Public unwillingness to provide the resources needed for prevention constitutes an act of passive tolerance of the abuse and neglect of children. Social factors in its etiology cannot be directly influenced by child protection professionals. Yet public elected officials have been granted the power to enact legislation and appropriate funds to reduce poverty, improve education, or implement other reforms that could decrease the potential of some parents to mistreat their children. Although it would be costly, the indignation usually expressed following the accounts of injuries and suffering inflicted on children by their parents may indicate growing public support for this broad approach. The current public investment in child protection is at best symbolic. Given the present scale of the problem, it may no longer purchase peace of mind.

Three previously presented recommendations are offered in view of current constraints. The principle constraint remains our failure to provide the funding required to protect children. We must not lose our grasp of the obvious. Well-conceived allocation of any resource is particularly important when that resource is in short supply. Careful consideration of environmental factors can improve the process by which child protection personnel are distributed geographically. But even their perfect allocation consistent with regional need will not solve the many problems which confront this country's child protection system. It is simply understaffed. Huge caseloads would be a part of daily life for workers even if equity of caseload could be achieved. Public commitment to increase dramatically the number of child protection workers in this country is long overdue. We may never completely rid ourselves of the mistreatment of our children, but expanding the number of professionals who endeavor to protect children can make a difference.

They succeed a child at a time, a frustrating reality given the monstrous dimensions of the problem.

Interest in evaluating the effectiveness of the U.S. child protection system increases with every media account of brutality to children. But all of the evaluation in the world can't reverse disappointing outcomes due to the inability of an assigned worker to dedicate sufficient time to a case. Evaluators must maintain an awareness of the difficulties faced by workers as they stand in judgment of their performance.

An analogy which may illuminate this need can be found in the results of drug studies conducted at health science centers throughout this country. Usually more than one dose of the experimental drug is used, along with a placebo for purposes of comparison. Typically, if the experimental drug is effective, it provides more relief, analgesic or curative effect, in large dosage than either its lower dose or the placebo medication. The child protection system can be likened to prescription of one or both of the two less efficacious drug regimens. Often the lower dose has no effect solely because it has been applied in insufficient quantity. It may, however, induce clinically undesirable side effects in the patient. The placebo merely creates the expectation on the part of the patient that relief is being provided.

To the extent that a shortage of personnel limits the capacity of the child protection system to advocate for children and serve the needs of abusive families, it is similar to insufficient dosage of a test drug, ineffective and even potentially harmful. And like the placebo medication, it creates expectation which cannot be fulfilled. For the evaluator of protective services, the dilemma is that in essence two control groups are being compared. There is no compelling reason to believe that the magnitude of response of our overburdened child protective system will yield satisfactory results, or for that matter, results substantially different from whose which occur in the absence of any intervention. For 153 children who died from their abuse, and undoubtedly thousands of others in the 18 study states who suffered revictimization, that investment was not enough.

Appendix A

Study	Consequences

Aber and Allen, 1987

    insecurity in relationships with adults
    reluctance to venture and explore

Adlolf, 1982

    negative self-concept
    low self-esteem
    difficult peer relationships
    difficult relationships with adults
    impaired capacity to trust

Altemeier, et. al., 1986

    feelings of being unwanted
    lower self-images
    isolation
    stress
    disturbed interpersonal relationships
    aggressive tendencies

Berliner and Wheeler, 1987
    anxiety

Blake-White and Kline, 1985

    post-traumatic stress syndrome (PTSD)
    dissociative hysteria
    acute anxiety
    suicidal ideation

Books, 1985

    depression
    hostility
    somatization
    paranoia

Study	Consequences

psychotic behaviors

Borgman, 1984

      suicide attempts
      running away

Briere and Runtz, 1987

      dissociation
      sleep disturbance
      tension
      anger
      suicide attempts
      substance addiction

Browne and Finkelhor, 1986

      depression
      self-destructive behavior
      anxiety
      isolation
      substance abuse
      sexual maladjustment
      hostility
      somatic disturbances
      emotional disturbance

Brunngraber, 1986

      emotional difficulties
      social difficulties
      self-identity problems
      familial problems
      interpersonal problems
      poor relationships with opposite sex
      sexuality problems

Burgess, 1986

      runaway
      feelings of alienation
      peer difficulties
      school difficulties
      anxiety

Study	Consequences

aggression
depression
prostitution

Burgess, 1985

anxiety
fear
self-blame
somatic problems
sexual development problems
sexual identity problems
phobic reactions
aggressive behavior
overly compliant behavior
poor peer relations
depression
regressive behaviors

Burgess, et. al., 1984

anxiety
distress
somatic complaints
acting out
erratic behavior
stress symptoms
non-responsiveness to environment

Cavaiola and Schiff, 1986

acting out
running away
sexual promiscuity

Coons, 1986

low self-esteem
self-mutilating behavior
suicidal behavior
guilt
cognitive disturbances
poor peer relationships
running away

Study	Consequences

poor body image
murderous behavior
intergenerational cycle of abuse
rape
prostitution

Cupoli, 1984

social skill development
language skill development
hyperactivity
poor impulse control
self-destructiveness
intergenerational cycle of abuse
running away
sexual dysfunction
difficult marital relationship

Daugherty, 1986

lower self-esteem
depression
sexual problems
interpersonal relationship problems

Daugherty, 1984

intergenerational cycle of abuse

Dean, et al., 1986

taking blame for actions of parent

Deighton and McPeek, 1985

guilt
anger
fear
early departure from family home
intergenerational cycle of abuse
flashbacks about sexual victimization

Study	Consequences

Donaldson, 1983

        low self-esteem
        difficulties in adult relationships

Donaldson and Gardner, 1985

        fear
        anxiety
        anger
        guilt
        self-disgust

Egeland, 1988

        severe developmental problems

Egeland, Sroufe and Erickson, 1983

        distractible
        lack of persistence
        lack of ego control
        lack of enthusiasm
        negative emotion

Farber and Joseph, 1985

        acting out
        depression
        generalized anxiety
        emotional disturbance
        helplessness
        dependency

Feldman, Mallouh and Lewis, 1986

        murderous behavior

Fielding, 1984

        emotional instability
        lack of self-confidence
        lack of self-respect
        fear of intimate relationships

Study	Consequences

Finkelhor and Browne, 1985

        traumas
        sexual dysfunction
        depression
        low self-esteem

Finkelhor and Browne, 1986

        inappropriate sexual attitudes
        shame
        guilt
        increased salience of sex
        confused sexual identity
        sexual dysfunction
        inappropriate sexual behaviors
        isolation
        substance abuse
        self-destructiveness
        delinquency
        somatic complaints

Fontana, 1984

        delinquency
        sexual abuse

Freeman-Longo, 1986

        intergenerational cycle of abuse

Garbarino, 1983

        aggressiveness

Garbarino, 1984

        developmental impairment
        delinquency
        psychiatric disorder

Garbarino and Plantz, 1984

        violent behavior

Study	Consequences

Goldfarb, 1987

      anorexia nervosa
      overeating

Goldwert, 1986

      problems with sexuality

Gomes-Schwartz, Horowitz and Sauzier, 1985
      psychological difficulties

Good and Rosenberg, 1984
      psychosocial dwarfism (PSD)

Green, 1985

      traumatic neurosis
      panic
      ego disorganization
      painful affective state

Harcourt, 1986

      sexual promiscuity
      depression
      running away
      suicidal behaviors
      helplessness
      intergeneration sexual abuse
      post-traumatic stress disorder (PTSD)

Harmon, Morgan and Glicken, 1984
      play lacks persistence
      play lacks quality
      motor retardation
      lack of interest in toys

Hart, Gelardo and Brassard, 1986
      failure-to-thrive
      developmental delays
      inappropriate behavior
      negative emotional affect
      interpersonal relationship problems

Study	Consequences

Herrenkohl, et al., 1984
social problems
emotional problems
poor interaction with parents

Howes and Espinosa, 1985
incompetent in peer interaction

Jacobsen, 1986

cognitive disturbances
affective disturbances
behavioral problems
running away
substance abuse
depression
post-traumatic stress disorder (PTSD)
personality disorders
relationship dysfunctions
psychosexual dysfunctions

Jaffe, et. al., 1986

internalization of problems
clinging to adults
loneliness
unhappiness
worrying
externalization of problems
disobedience
lying
cheating
cruelty to others
fighting

Janus, Burgess and McCormack, 1987
running away
delinquency
depression
tension
low self-image

Study	Consequences

Johnson and Shrier, 1987

        sexual dysfunction
        homosexuality

Johnson and Shrier, 1985

        homosexuality
        bisexuality
        nonorganic sexual dysfunction

Jones, 1984

        emotional disorders
        conduct disorders
        anxiety
        teen pregnancy
        running away
        social withdrawal
        self-destructiveness
        school failure
        depression
        inappropriate sexual behavior
        intergenerational sexual abuse
        sexual dysfunction

Kempe and Kempe, 1984

        feelings of vulnerability
        shame
        guilt
        poor self-image

Korbin, 1986

        intergenerational cycle of abuse

Krener, 1985

        post-traumatic stress disorder (PTSD)
        psychiatric symptoms
        nightmares
        phobias
        low self-esteem

Study	Consequences

Krugman, 1985

        behavior problems
        cognitive developmental delay

Lancet, 1986

        depression
        feelings of helplessness

Landa, 1984

        stunted psychological growth
        no sense of individualized identity

Leehan and Wilson, 1985

        low self-esteem
        poor interpersonal skills
        helplessness
        sexual disorders
        nightmares

Lewis, et al., 1985

        murderous behavior
        psychotic symptoms
        violent childhood acts

Lindberg and Distad, 1985

        post-traumatic stress disorder (PTSD)

MacFarlane, 1985

        self-blame
        fear
        guilt
        anger
        anxiety

Maller, 1984

        prostitution

Study	Consequences

McCord, 1983

juvenile delinquency
alcoholism
mental illness

McCormack, Burgess and Janus, 1986

running away
anxiety
suicidal feelings
pysical symptomatology
fear
confusion about sex
delinquency

McFaddin, 1982

appetite loss
bedwetting
sleep disturbances

Middleton, 1984

depression
confusion of sexuality
confusion of affection
poor self-esteem
disassociation
somatic complaints
substance abuse
eating disorder
guilt
intergenerational sexual abuse
destructive relationship patterns
loneliness

Monopolis and Sarles, 1985

emotional growth impeded
intergenerational cycle of abuse
violent behavior
prostitution
multiple personality
depression

Study	Consequences

lack of basic trust
anxiety
aggressiveness

Mouzakitis, 1984

acting out behaviors
delinquency

Nash and West, 1985

unhappiness
early overt sexual behavior
adult scxual dissatisfaction

O'Brien, 1987

adjustment disorder
developmental problems
isolation problems
damaged self-esteem
body image problems
no sense of control over environment

Oates, 1986

cognitive deficits
behavior problems
lack of trust
low self-esteem
pathological development

Oates, Peacock and Forrest, 1984
language developmentally delayed
verbal intelligence deficit

Oliver, 1985

personality disorders
suicide attempts
mental handicaps
substance abuse
epilepsy
inappropriate sexual behavior

Study	Consequences
	antisocial behavior
	intergenerational cycle of abuse
Putnam and Stein, 1985	
	suicidal behavior
	suicide ideation
	self-mutilation
Putnam, et al., 1986	
	multiple personality disorders (MPD)
	depression
	dissociative symptoms
Rosenfeld, 1987	
	borderline personalities
	multiple personalities
Runtz and Briere, 1986	
	delinquent teenage behaviors
	conflict with authority
	early sexual behavior
	eating problems
Ruskin, 1984	
	self-blame
	guilt
	fear
	revulsion
	nightmares
	bedwetting
Salter, Richardson and Kairys, 1985	
	cognitive skills deficits
	affective disturbances
	aggressiveness
	withdrawal

Study	Consequences

Sandberg, 1986

        acting out behaviors
        self-mutilation
        suicide

Schaffer and DeBlassie, 1984
        prostitution

Schecter, Schwartz, and Greenfield, 1987
        anorexia nervosa

Skuse, 1984

        retardation
        poor language skill development
        paucity of emotion expression
        lack of attachment behavior
        social withdrawal

Snyder, Hampton and Newberger, 1983
        cognitive developmental delay
        emotional problems
        physical trauma
        language developmental delay
        poor self-concept
        poor social relations
        pseudomaturity
        aggression

Steele, 1987

        poor sense of self
        shaky identity
        lack of basic trust in people
        difficulty in finding pleasure
        propensity for depression
        fears of intimacy
        feelings of emptiness
        dependency

Study	Consequences

Steele, 1986

    intergenerational cycle of abuse
    inability to derive pleasure
    low self-esteem
    identity problems
    diminished coping ability
    depression
    destructive life patterns
    delinquency
    psychiatric problems
    relationship problems
    sexuality problems

Strother, 1986

    depression
    personality problems

Stuart and Allen, 1984

    self-mutilation
    anorexia nervosa

Summit, 1985

    helplessness
    diminished self-worth
    precocious sexual interest
    indiscrete masturbatory activity
    social withdrawal
    underachievement
    low self-esteem
    somatic complaints

Thomas and Rogers, 1984

    psychomatic problems
    enuresis
    encopresis
    somatic complaints
    interpersonal relationship problems
    aggression
    sexual misconduct
    withdrawal

Study	Consequences
	temper tantrums
Tong, Oates and McDowell, 1987	less confident fewer friends
	aggressive increased sexual awareness lower self-esteem
Walters, 1986	psychological damage poor self-image poor emotional development poor moral development
Wilbur, 1984	multiple personality disorder (MPD)
Winestine, 1985	feelings of helplessness feelings of worthlessness
Wolfgang, 1982	intergenerational cycle of abuse poor self-esteem incapacity to enjoy life
Young, 1984	phobia anxiety fear phobia

References

Aber, J. L., & Allen, J. P. (1987). Effects of maltreatment on young children's young children's socioemotional development: An attachment theory perspective. *Developmental Psychology*, *23*(3), 486-414.

Adolf, J. W. (1982). Emotional consequences of child abuse: The attachment relationship. Washington: Educational Resources Information Center.

Albee, G. W. (1988). Primary prevention and social problems. In G. Gerbner et al. (Eds.), *Child abuse: An agenda for action*. New York: Oxford University Press.

Altemeier, W. A., Sherrod, K. B., O'Connor, S., & Tucker, D. (1986). Outcome of abuse during childhood among pregnant low income women. *Child Abuse and Neglect*, *10*(3), 319-330.

American Humane Association. (n.d.). *Trends in child abuse and neglect: national perspective*. Denver: American Humane Association

Anderson, R., Ambrosino, R., Valentine, D. & Lauderdale, M. (1983). Child deaths attributed to abuse and neglect: An empirical study. *Children and Youth Services Review*, *5*(1), 75-89

Aneshensel, C. S., & Huba, G. J. (1983). Depression, alcohol use, and smoking over one year. *Journal of Abnormal Psychology*, *92*(2), 124-150.

Antler, S. (1978). Child abuse: An emerging social priority. *Social Work*, *23*(1), 58-61.

Antler, S. The rediscovery of child abuse. (1981). In L. H. Pelton, (Ed.), *The social context of child abuse and neglect*. New York: Human Sciences Press.

Antler, S. *Child abuse and child protection: Policy and practice*. (1982). Silver Spring, Md.: National Association of Social Workers.

Antler, S. (1983). Preventing child abuse and neglect: Issues and problems. (1983). In N. B. Ebeling & D. A. Hill (Eds.), *Child abuse and neglect: A guide with case studies for treating the child and family*. Littleton, Mass.: John Wright-PSG, Inc.

Armstrong, K. L. (1979). How to avoid burnout: A study of the relationship between burnout and worker: Organizational and management characteristics in eleven child abuse and neglect projects. *Child Abuse and Neglect*, *3*, 135-149.

Arnold, E. (1982). The use of corporal punishment in child rearing in the West Indies. *Child Abuse and Neglect*, *6*(2), 141-145.

Ayoub, C. & Pfeifer, D. (1979). Burns as a manifestation of child abuse and neglect. *American Journal of Diseases of Children, 133*(9), 910-914.

Bagley, C. (1984). Mental health and the in-family sexual abuse of children and adolescents. *Canada's Mental Health, 32*(2), 17-23.

Baily, W., & Baily, T. (1985). Etiology of neglect. In C. Mouzakitis & R. Varghese (Eds.), *Social work treatment with abused and neglected children.* Springfield, Ill.: Charles C. Thomas Publisher.

Baker, J. M. (1982) Psychological and sociological aspects of child abuse. In A. M. Haralambie (Ed.), *Practical child advocacy.* Denver: National Association of Counsel for Children.

Baldwin, J. A. (1977). Child abuse: Epidemiology and prevention. In P. J. Graham (Ed.), *Epidemiological approaches in child pscyhiatry.* New York: Academic Press.

Baldwin, W. (1983). Trends in adolescent contraception, pregnancy, and child bearing. In E. R. McAnarney (Ed.), *Premature adolescent pregnancy and parenthood.* New York: Grune and Stratton.

Bandura, A. (1977). *Social learning theory.* Englewood Cliffs, N.J.: Prentice-Hall.

Becker, J. V., Kaplan, M. S., Cunningham-Rathner, J., & Kavoussi, R. (1986). Characteristics of adolescent sexual perpetrators: Preliminary findings. *Journal of Family Violence, 1*(1), 85-97.

Benedict, M. I., & White, R. B. (1985). Selected perinatal factors and child abuse. *American Journal of Public Health, 75*(7), 780-781.

Bennett, A. N., & Pethybridge, R. (1979). A study of abused children on the Gosport (Hampshire) Peninsula. *Journal of the Royal Society of Medicine, 72*(10), 743-747.

Berliner, L., & Wheeler, J. R. (1987). Treating the effects of sexual abuse on children. *Journal of Interpersonal Violence, 2*(4), 415-434.

Besharov, D., & Besharov, S. (1977, Winter). Why do parents harm their children? *National Council of Jewish Women,* pp. 6-8.

Billingsley, A. (1980). *Black families at risk: National policies and systemic influences contributing to the phenomenon.* Baltimore: National Resource Center on Child Abuse and Neglect for Urban Black Families.

Blake, R. L., Jr. (1988). The effects of stress and social support on health: A research challenge for family medicine. *Family Medicine, 20,* 19-24.

Blake-White, J., & Kline, C. M. (1985). Treating the dissociative process in adult victims of childhood incest. *Social Casework, 66*(7), 394-402.

Blampied, P. (1978). In Massachusetts: A hotline to tragedy. *Time, 112,* 6-7.

Blau, P. M. and Duncan, O. D. (1967). *The American occupational structure.* New York: John Wiley & Sons, Inc.

Blumberg, M. L. (1974). Psychopathology of the abusing parent. *American Journal of Psychotherapy, 28,* 21-29.

Bolton, F. G. (1981). *Child maltreatment and the adolescent parent: Balancing the social, environmental, and individual factors*. National Family Violence Research Conference. Durham, New Hampshire.

Borgman, R. (1984, March). Problems of sexually abused girls and their treatment. *Social Casework*, pp. 182-186.

Briere, J., & Runtz, M. (1987). Post sexual abuse trauma: Data and implications for clinical practice. *Journal of Interpersonal Violence*, *2*(4), 367-379.

Bronfenbrenner, U. (1977). Toward an experimental ecology of human development. *American Psychologist*, *32*, 513-531.

Bronfenbrenner, U. (1978). Who needs parent education? *Teachers College Record*, *79*, 767-787.

Bronfenbrenner, U. (1979). Reality and research in the ecology of human development. In D. G. Gil (Ed.), *Child abuse and violence*. New York: Ams Press.

Browne, A. & Finkelhor, D. (1986). Impact of child sexual abuse: A review of the research. *Psychological Bulletin*, *99*(1),66-77.

Brunngraber, L. S. (1986). Father-daughter incest: Immediate and long-term effects of sexual abuse. *Advances in Nursing Science*, *8*(4), 15-35.

Bunney, W., Jr., Shapito, A., Adler, R., Davis, J., Herd, A., Kopin, I., Krieger, D. Matthyse, S., Stunkard, A., & Weissman, M. (1982). Panel report on stress and illness. In G. R. Elliott & C. Eisdorfer (Ed.) *Stress and human health*. New York: Springer Publishing.

Burgess, A. W. (1985). The sexual victimization of adolescents. Washington: Government Printing Office.

Burgess, A. W. (1986). *Youth at risk: Understanding runaway and exploited youth*. Washington: National Center for Missing and Exploited Children.

Burgess, A. W., Hartman, C. R., McCausland, M. P., & Powers, P. (1984). Impact of child pornography and sex rings on child victims and their families. In A. W. Burgess (Ed.). *Child pornography and sex rings*. Lexington, Mass.: Lexington Books.

Calam, R. & Franchi, C. (1987). Child abuse and its consequences: Observational approaches. Cambridge: Cambridge University Press.

Cameron, J. M. (1977). The battered baby. *British Journal of Hospital Medicine*, *4*, 769-777.

Caplan, P. J., Watters, J., White, G., Perry, R., & Bates, R. Toronto multiagency child abuse research project: The abused and abuser. *Child Abuse and Neglect*, *8*, 343-351.

Cappell, C. L. & Mays, K. L. (1973). *The correlated structure of child abuse: Advances toward a social indicator model*. Washington: Educational Resources Information Center.

Card, J. J. & Wise, L. L. (1978). Teenage mothers and teenage fathers: The impact of early child bearing on the parents' personal and professional lives. *Family Planning Perspectives* 10, 199-204.

Carter, G. W. (1980). Measurement of need. In N. A. Polansky (Ed.), *Social work research*. Chicago: University of Chicago Press.

Cavaiola, A. A., & Schiff, M. (1986). *Behavioral sequelae of physical and/or sexual abuse in adolescents*. International Congress of Child and Adolescent Psychiatry and Allied Professions 11th Meeting. Paris.

Cazenave, N. A., & Straus, M. A. (1979). Race, class, network embeddedness and family violence: A search for potent support systems. *Journal of Comparative Family Studies, 10* (3), 280-299.

Ceresine, S. J., & Starr, R. H. (1977). *Child abuse: A controlled study of social and family factors*. American Psychological Association, 85th Annual meeting, San Francisco, California.

Chesser, E. (1952). *Cruelty to children*. New York: Philosophical Library.

Chunn, J. (1980). *An exploratory investigation of potential societal and intra-familial factors contributing to child abuse and neglect*. Washington: National Council for Black Child Development.

Clausen, J. A., & Kohn, M. L. (1954). The analysis of ecological and statistical distributions of personality variables. *American Journal of Sociology, 60*, 140-151.

Cohn, A. H. (1979. Effective treatment of child abuse and neglect. *Social Work, 24*, 513-519.

Coles, R. (1979). *Violence in ghetto children*. In D. G. Gil (Ed.), *Child abuse and violence*. New York: AMS Press.

Colorado Department of Social Services. (1986). *Reporting of child abuse b Colorado central registry*. Denver: Colorado Department of Social Services.

Cooley, C. H. (1930). *Sociological theory and social research*. New York: Henry Holt and Co.

Coons, P. M. (1986). Psychiatric problems associated with child abuse: A review. In J. J. Jacobsen (Ed.), *Psychiatric sequelae of child abuse*. Springfield, Ill.: Charles C. Thomas.

Court, J. (1975). Nurture and nature: The nurturing problem. In A. W. Franklin (Ed.), *Concerning child abuse*. Edinburgh, Scotland: Churchill Livingstone.

Creighton, S. J. (1979). An epidemiological study of child abuse. *Child Abuse and Neglect, 3*(2), 601-605.

Cupoli, J. M. (1984). Consequences of child abuse. In D. C. Bross (Ed.), *Multidisciplinary advocacy for mistreated children*. Denver: National Association of Counsel for Children.

Daley, M. R. (1979). Burnout: Smouldering problem in protective services. *Social Work, 24*, 375-379.

Daugherty, L. B. (1984). *Why me? Help for victims of child sexual abuse.* Racine, Wis.: Mother Courage Press.

Daugherty, L. B. (1986). What happens to victims of child sexual abuse? In M. Nelson & K. Clark (Eds.), *The educator's guide to preventing child sexual abuse.* Santa Cruz, Calif.: Network Publications.

Dean, A. L., Malik, M. M., Richards, W., & Stringer, S.(1986). Effects of parental maltreatment on children's conceptions of interpersonal relationships. *Developmental Psychology, 22*(5), 617-626.

Deighton, J., & McPeek, P. (1985). Group treatment: adult victims of childhood sexual abuse. *Social Casework, 66*(7), 403-420.

Delsordo, J. (1963). Protective casework for abused children. *Children, 10,* 213-218.

Denver Research Institute. (1974). *Analysis and synthesis of needs assessment research in the field of human services.* Denver: University of Denver.

Denver Research Institute. (1981). *The national study on child neglect and abuse reporting.* Volume I: *User documentation.* Denver: American Humane Association.

de Silva, W. (1981). Some cultural and economic factors leading to neglect, abuse and violence in respect of children within the family in Sri Lanka. *Child Abuse and Neglect, 5*(4), 391-405.

Dibble, U. (1982). Child abuse and neglect: Survey essays. *Contemporary Sociology, 11*(4), 388-390.

Dibble, U., & Straus, M. A. (1980). Some social structure determinants of inconsistency between attitudes and behavior: The case of family violence. *Journal of Marriage and the Family, 42*(1), 71-80.

Dilorenzo, P. (1978). *Abuse in the lower socio-economic family: Implications for the planner.* Annual National Conference on Child Abuse and Neglect, New York.

Donaldson, M. A. (1983). *Incest, years after: Putting the pain to rest.* Fargo, N.D.: The Village Family Service Center.

Donaldson, M. A., & Gardner, R. (1985). Diagnosis and treatment of traumatic stress among women after childhood incest. In C. R. Figley (Ed.), *Trauma and its wake: The study and treatment of post-traumatic stress disorders.* New York: Brunner-Mazel Publishers.

Downing, L. C. (1980). *A comparative analysis of the incidence, type and trends of child abuse.* Doctoral dissertation, University of Michigan.

Duncan, G., Hill, M., & Rogers, W. (1986). The changing fortunes of young and old. *American Demographics,* pp. 27-33.

Duncan, O. D., Cuzzort, R. P., & Duncan, B. (1961). *Statistical geography.* Glencoe, Ill.: The Free Press.

Dunham, H. W. (1947). The current status of ecological research in mental disorder. *Social Forces, 24,* 321-326.

Duran, B. J., & Bernotas, T. (1981). Family migration: Minimizing community costs, maximizing community benefits. In *Proceedings of the Fifth National Conference on Child Abuse and Neglect*. Milwaukee: Region V Child Abuse and Neglect Resource Center.

Durkheim, E. (1951). *Suicide*. Trans. J. A. Spaulding & G.Simpson. Glencoe, Ill.: Free Press.

Education Commission of the States. (1979). *Trends in child protection laws--1979*. Denver: Education Commission of the States.

Egeland, B. (1988). The consequences of physical and emotional neglect on the development of young children. In *Child neglect monograph: Proceedings from a symposium*. Washington: Clearinghouse on Child Abuse and Neglect Information (DHHS).

Egeland, B., Breitenbucher, M., & Rosenberg, D. (1980). Prospective study of the significance of life stress in the etiology of child abuse. *Journal of Consulting and Clinical Psychology*, *48*(2), 195-205.

Elmer, E. (1981). Traumatized children, chronic illness, and poverty. In L. H. Pelton (Ed.), *The social context of child abuse and neglect*. New York: Human Sciences Press.

Epstein, A. S. (19). *Assessing the child developmentinformation needed by adolescent parents with very young children*. Final report of the High/Scope Educational Research Foundation to the Office of Child Development, DHEW.

Farber, E. D., & Joseph, J. A. (1985). The maltreated adolescent: Patterns of physical abuse. *Child Abuse and Neglect*, *9*(2), 201-206.

Faris, R. (1944). Ecological factors in human behavior. In J. McV. Hunt (Ed.), *Personality and the behavior disorders*. New York: Ronald Press.

Faris, R. (1967). *Chicago Sociology: 1920-1932*. San Francisco: Chandler Publishing Co.

Faris, R., & Dunham, H. (1939). *Mental disorders in urban areas*. Chicago: University of Chicago Press.

Fauri, D. P. (1978). Points and viewpoints protecting the child protective service worker. *Social Work*, *23*, 62-64.

Featherman, D. L., & Hauser, R. M. (1978). *Opportunity and change*. New York: Academic Press.

Feldman, M., Mallouh, K., & Lewis, D. O. (1986). Filicidal abuse in the histories of 15 condemned murderers. *Bulletin of the American Academy of Psychiatry and the Law*, *14*(4), 345-352.

Fergusson, D. M., Fleming, J., & O'Neill, D. P. (1972). *Child abuse in New Zealand*. Wellington, New Zealand: Department of Social Welfare.

Fielding, B. (1984). I was a victim of incest. *Victimology 9*(1), 5-8.

Finkelhor, D. (1982). Sexual abuse: A sociological perspective. *Child Abuse and Neglect*, *6*(l), 95-102.

Finkelhor, D. (1986). *A sourcebook on child sexual abuse*. Beverly Hills, California: Sage Publications.

Finkelhor, D., & Browne, A. (1985). The traumatic impact of child sexual abuse: A conceptualization. *American Journal of Orthopsychiatry, 55*(4), 530-541.

Finkelhor, D., & Browne, A. (1986). Initial and long-term effects: A conceptual framework. In D. Finkelhor (Ed.), *A sourcebook on child sexual abuse*. Beverly Hills, Calif.: Sage Publications, Inc.

Fitch, F. J., & Papantonio. (1983). Men who batter: Some pertinent characteristics. *Journal of Nervous and Mental Disease, 171*(3), 190-293.

Fontana, V. (1977, April 6-7). Statement printed in Senate hearings on extension of the Child Abuse Prevention and Treatment Act, p. 505.

Fontana, V. (1984). Child abuse, past, present and future. *Human Ecology Forum, 15*(1), 5-7.

Fraley, Y. L. (1983). The family support center: Early intervention high-risk parents and children. *Children Today, 12*(1), 13-17.

Fraser, B. (1976-1977). Independent representation for the abused and neglected child: The guardian ad litem. *California Western Law Review*, p. 13.

Fraser, G., & Kilbride, P. O. (1980). Child abuse and neglect--rare, but perhaps increasing phenomen among the Samia of Kenya. *Child Abuse and Neglect, 4*(4), 227-232.

Freedman, A. M., Kaplan, H. I., & Sadock, B. J. (1972). *Modern synopsis of psychiatry*. Baltimore: The Williams & Wilkins Co.

Freeman-Longo, R. E. (1986). Impact of sexual victimization on males. *Child Abuse and Neglect, 10*(3), 411-414.

Freud, S. (1950). *Collected papers*. Vol. 2. London: Hogarth.

Friedrich, W. N., & Einbender, A. J. (1983). The abused child: A psychological review. *Journal of Clinical Child Psychology, 12*(3), 244-256.

Friedrich, W. N., & Wheller, K. K. (1982). The abusing parent revisited: A decade of psychological research. *Journal of Nervous and Mental Disease, 170*(10), 577-587.

Fryer, G. E., Jr., Poland, J. E., Bross, D. C., & Krugman, R. D. (1988). The child protective service worker: A profile of needs, attitudes, and utilization of professional resources. *Child Abuse and Neglect, 12*, 481-490.

Fryer, G. E., Jr., Miyoshi, T. J., & Thomas, P. J. (1989). The relationship of child protection worker attitudes to attrition from the field. *Child Abuse and Neglect, 13*, 345-350.

Fryer, G. E., Jr. (1990). Detecting and reporting child abuse: A function of the human service delivery system. *Journal of Sociology and Social Welfare, 17*(2), 143-157.

Gagan, R. J., Cupoli, J. M., & Watkins, A. H. (1984). The families of children who fail to thrive. *Child Abuse and Neglect, 8*(1), 93-203.

Galdston, R. (1965). Observations of children who have been physically abused by their parents. *American Journal of Psychiatry, 122*(4), 440-443.

Galdston, R. (1979). Preventing the abuse of little children: The parents' center project for the study and prevention of child abuse. In D. G. Gil (Ed.), *Child abuse and violence.* New York: AMS Press.

Garbarino, J. (1976). A preliminary study of some ecological correlates of child abuse: The impact of socioeconomic stress on mothers. *Child Development, 47,* 178-185.

Garbarino, J. (1980). What kind of society permits child abuse? *Infant Mental Health Journal, 1*(4), 270-280.

Garbarino, J. (1981). An ecological approach to child maltreatment. In L. H. Pelton (Ed.), *The social context of child abuse and neglect.* New York: Human Sciences Press.

Garbarino, J. (1983). *The link between child abuse and juvenile delinquency.* Senate Subcommittee Hearing to Examine the Relationship Between Child Abuse and Neglect, Juvenile Delinquency and Adult Criminality.

Garbarino, J. (1984). What have we learned about child maltreatment? In *Perspective on child maltreatment in the mid 80's.* Washington: National Center on Child Abuse and Neglect.

Garbarino, J., & Plantz, M. C. (1984). An ecological perspective on the outcomes of child maltreatment: What difference will the differences make? In D. C. Bross (Ed.), *Multidisciplinary advocacy for mistreated children.*

Garbarino, J., & Sherman, D. (1980). Identifying high-risk neighborhoods. In J. Garbarino and H. Stocking (Eds.), *Protecting children from abuse and neglect.* San Francisco: Jossey Bass Publishers.

Garbarino, J., & Stocking, S. H. (1980). *Protecting children from abuse and neglect.* San Francisco: Jossey-Bass Publishers.

Garbarino, J., Sherman, D., & Crouter, A. C. (1979). Assessing the neighborhood context of child maltreatment. *Child Abuse and Neglect, 3*(304), 1049-1069.

Gaudin, J. M., Jr. (1979). *Mothers' perceived strength of primary group networks and maternal child abuse.* Doctoral dissertation.

Gelles, R. J. (1985). Family violence: What we know and can do. In E. H. Newberger & R. Bourne (Eds.), *Unhappy families.* Littleton, Mass.: PSG Publishing Co.

Germain, C. B. (1982). Child welfare in the 80's - will the graduate level curriculum prepare the MSW? In E. Saalberg (Ed.), *A dialogue on the challenge for education and training.* Ann Arbor, Mich.: National Welfare Training Center.

122

Gil, D. G. (1969). Physical abuse of children: Findings and implications of a nationwide survey. *Pediatrics, 44* (Supplement): 857-864.

Gil, D. G. (1970). *Violence against children.* Cambridge, Mass.: Harvard University Press.

Gil, D. G. (1975). Unraveling child abuse. *American Journal of Ortho-psychiatry, 45,* 346-356.

Gil, D. G. (1977). Child abuse: Levels of manifestation, causal dimensions, and primary prevention. *Victimology, 2*(2),186-194.

Gil, D. G. (Ed.). (1979). *Child abuse and violence.* New York: AMS Press.

Gil, D. G. (1981). The United States versus child abuse. In L. H. Pelton (Ed.), *The social context of child abuse and neglect.* New York: Human Sciences Press.

Gil, D. G. (1985). The political and economic context of child abuse. In E. H. Newberger and R. Bourne (Eds.). *Unhappy families.* Littleton, Mass.: PSG Publishing Co.

Giovannoni, J., & Billingsley, A. (1970). Child neglect among the poor: A study of parental inadequacy in families of three ethnic groups. *Child Welfare, 49,* 196-204.

Goldfarb, L. (1987). Sexual abuse antecedent to anorexia nervosa, bulimia, and compulsive overeating: Three case reports. *International Journal of Eating Disorders, 6*(5), 675-680.

Goldwert, M. (1986). Childhood seduction and the spiritualization of psychology: The case of Jung and Rank. *Child Abuse and Neglect, 10*(4), 555-557.

Gomes-Schwartz, B., Horowitz, J. M., & Sauzier, M. (1985). Severity of emotional distress among sexually abused preschool, school-age, and adolescent children. *Hospital and Community Psychiatry, 36*(5), 503-508.

Good, W. V., & Rosenberg, D. (1984). Psychosocial dwarfism: Review and case reports. In D. C. Bross (Ed.), *Multidisciplinary advocacy for mistreated children.* Denver: National Association of Counsel for Children.

Gray, C. L. (1978). *Empathy and stress as mediators in child abuse: Theory, research and practice implications.* Doctoral dissertation.

Green, A. H. (1985). Generational transmission of violence in child abuse. *International Journal of Family Psychiatry, 6*(4), 389-403.

Green, A. H. (1976). A psychodynamic approach to the study and treatment of child-bearing parents. *Journal of the Academy of Child Psychiatry, 15,* 414-429.

Guttmacher Institute. (1981). *Teenage pregnancy: The problem that hasn't gone away.* New York: Guttmacher Institute.

Harcourt, M. (1986). Child sexual abuse. In J. J. Jacobson (Ed.), *Psychiatric sequelae of child abuse.* Springfield, Ill.: Charles C. Thomas.

Harmon, R. J., Morgan, G. A., & Glicken, A. D. (1984). Continuities and discontinuities in affective and cognitive-mional development. *Child Abuse and Neglect, 8*(2), 157-167.

Harrison, W. D. (1980). Role strain and burnout in child protective services. *Social Services Review, 54* 31-44.

Hart, S. N., Gelardo, M., & Brassard, M. (1986). Psychological maltreatment. In J. J. Jacobson (Ed.), *Psychiatric sequelae of child abuse.* Springfield, Ill.: Charles C. Thomas.

Helfer, R. E. (1973). The etiology of child abuse. *Pediatrics, 51,* 777.

Helfer, R. E. (1982). A review of the literature on the prevention of child abuse and neglect. *Child Abuse and Neglect, 6,* 251-261.

Henry, D. R. (1978). The psychological aspects of child abuse. In S. M. Smith (Ed.), *The maltreatment of children.* Baltimore: University Park Press.

Hergenroeder, A. C., Taylor, P. M., Rogers, R. D., & Taylor, F. (1985). Neonatal characteristics of maltreated infants and children. *American Journal of Diseases of Children, 139*(3), 295-298.

Hollingshead, A. B., & Redlich, F. C. (1953). Social stratification and psychiatric disorders. *American Sociological Review, 18,* 163-169.

Holman, R. R., & Kanwar, S. (1975). Early life of the battered child. *Archives of Disease in Childhood, 50*(1), 78-80.

Holmes, T. H., & Rahe, R. H. (1974). *Life stress and illness.* Springfield, Ill.: Charles C. Thomas.

Horowitz, B., & Wolock, I. (1981). Material deprivation, child maltreatment, and agency interventions among poor families. In L. H. Pelton (Ed.), *The social context of child abuse and neglect.* New York: Human Sciences Press.

Jacobsen, J. J. (1986). *Psychiatric sequelae of child abuse.* Springfield, Ill.: Charles C. Thomas.

Jaffe, P., Wolfe, D., Wilson S., & Zak, L. (1986). Similarities in behavioral and social maladjustment among child victims and witnesses to family violence. *American Journal of Orthopsychiatry, 56*(1), 142-146.

Jameson, P. A., & Schellenbach, C. J. (1977). Sociological and psychological factors in the backgrounds of male and female perpetrators of child abuse. *Child Abuse and Neglect, 1*(1), 77-83.

Janus, M., Burgess, A. W., & McCormack, A. (1087). Histories of sexual abuse in adolescent male runaways. *Adolescence, 22*(86), 405-417.

Jason, J. (1983). Child homicide spectrum. *American Journal of Diseases of Children, 137*(6), 578-581.

Jayaratne, S., Chess, W. A., & Kunkel, D. A. (1986). Burnout: Its impact on child welfare workers and their spouses. *Social Work, 31,* 53-59.

124

Jenkins, C. S. (1976). Recent evidence supporting psychologic and social risk factors for coronary disease. *New England Journal of Medicine, 294* 987-994.

Johnson, R. L., & Shrier, D. (1987). Past sexual victimization by females of male patients in an adolescent medicine clinic population. *American Journal of Psychiatry, 144*(5), 650-652.

Jones, D. (1984). Interviewing the sexually abused child: I - The Clinical background. In D. C. Bross (Ed.), Multidisciplinary advocacy for mistreated children. Denver: National Association of Counsel for Children.

Justice, B., & Calvert, A. (1985). Factors mediating child abuse as a response to stress. *Child Abuse and Neglect, 9*(3), 359-363.

Justice, B., & Justice, R. (1982). Etiology of physical abuse of children and dynamics of coercive treatment. In J. C. Hansen & L. R. Barnhill (Eds.), *Clinical approaches to family violence.* Rockville, Md.: Aspen Systems Corp.

Kahn, A. J. (1969). *Theory and practice of social planning.* New York: Russell Sage Foundation.

Kahn, R. (1978). Job burnout prevention and remedies. *Public Welfare, 36,* 61-63.

Kaplan, Abraham. (1964). *The conduct of inquiry.* San Francisco: Chandler Publishing Co.

Kaplun, D., & Reich, R. (1976). The murdered child and his killers. *American Journal of Psychiatry, 133*(7), 809-813.

Kasl, S. V. (1984). Stress and health. *Annual Review of Public Health, 5,* 319-342.

Kelly, J. A. (1983). *Treating child-abusive families.* New York: Plenum Press.

Kempe, C. H., Silverman, F. N., Steele, B. F., Drogenmueller, W., & Silver, H. K. (1962). The battered child syndrome. *Journal of the American Medical Association, 181,* 17-24.

Kempe, C. H., & Helfer, R. E. (1972). *Helping the battered child and his family.* Philadelphia: Lippincott.

Kempe, R. S., & Kempe, C. H. (1984). *The common secret: Sexual abuse of children and adolescents.* New York: W. H. Freeman and Co.

Kenniston, D. (1979). Do Americans really like children? In D. G. Gil (Ed.), *Child abuse and violence.* New York: Ams Press.

Kent, J., Weisberg, H., Lamar, F., & Marx, T. (1983). Understanding the etiology of child abuse: A preliminary typology of cases. *Children and Youth Services Review, 5*(1), 7-29.

Kinard. E. M., & Klerman, L. (1980). Teenage parenting and child abuse: Are they related? *American Journal of Orthopsychiatry, 509*3), 481-488.

Klecka, W. R. (1980). *Discriminant analysis.* Beverly Hills: Sage.

Kohn, M. (1969). *Class and conformity.* Homewood, Illinois: The Dorsey Press.

Korbin, J. E. (1986). Childhood histories of women imprisoned for fatal child maltreatment. *Child Abuse and neglect, 10*(3), 331-338.

Krener, P. (1985). Clinical experience - after incest: Secondary prevention? *Journal of the American Academy of Child Psychiatry, 24*(2), 231-234.

Krugman, R. D. (1984). Relation between unemployment and physical abuse of children. In D. C. Bross (Ed.), *Multidisciplinary advocacy for mistreated children.* Denver: National Association for Counsel for Children.

Lacayo, R. (1987). Sexual abuse or abuse of justice? *Time, 129*, p. 49.

Lancet. (1986). Childhood depression and sexual abuse. *Lancet, 1*(8474), 196.

Landa, S. (1984). *Child abuse in cults.* Fifth International Conference on Child Abuse and Neglect, Montreal.

Larson, O. W., Doris, J., & Alvarez, W. F. (1984). *Child maltreatment among migrant farmworkers: Findings from the eastern stream incidence study.* International Congress on CHild Abuse and Neglect, Montreal.

Last, J. M. (1983). *A dictionary of epidemiology.* New York: Oxford University Press.

Lawrence, R. A. McAnarney, E. R., & Aten, M. J. (1981). Aggressive behaviors in young mothers: Markers of future morbidity? *Pediatric Research, 15*, 443.

Leehan, J., & Wilson, L. P. (1985). *Grown-up abused children.* Springfield, Ill.: Charles C. Thomas.

Leonard, M. F., Rhymes, I. P., & Solnit, A. J. (1966). Failure to thrive in infants. *American Journal of Diseases of Children, 111*(6), 600-612.

Lewis, D. O., Moy, E., Jackson, L. D., Aaronson, R., & Restifo, N. (1985). Biopsychosocial characteristics of children who later murder: A prospective study. *American Journal of Psychiatry, 142*(10), 1161-1167.

Lieberson, S. (1985). *Making it count: The improvement of social research and theory.* Berkeley: University of California Press.

Lindberg, F. H., & Distad, L. J. (1985). Post-traumatic stress disorders in women who experienced childhood incest. *Child Abuse and Neglect, 9*(3), 329-334.

Leoning, W. E. (1981). Child abuse among the Zulus: a people in cultural transition. *Child Abuse and Neglect, 5*(1), 3-7.

Lowery, E. (1978). *The social context of child abuse.* Annual National Conference on Child Abuse and Neglect, New York.

Lynch, M. A., & Roberts, J. (1977). Predicting child abuse: Signs of bonding failure in the maternity hospital. *British Medical Journal, 1*, 624-626.

126

MacFarlane, K. (1985). *Please, no, not my child . . . coping with abuse of your preschool child*. Los Angeles, Calif: Child Sexual Abuse Diagnostic Center.

MacMahon, B., Pugh, T. F., & Ipsen, J. (1970). *Epidemiologic methods*. Boston: Little, Brown and Co.

Madge, N. (1983). Unemployment and its effects on children. *Journal of Child Psychology and Psychiatry and Allied Disciplines, 24*(2), 311-319.

Maller, P. (1984). From prostitution to child sex abuse prevention. *Victimology, 9*(3-4), 318-320.

Margolis, L. H., & Farran, D. C. (1984). Unemployment and children. *International Journal of Mental Health, 13*(1-2), 107-124.

Martin, M. P., & Klaus, S. L. (1979). *Worker burnout among child protective service workers*. Washington: National Center on Child Abuse and Neglect.

Maslach, C. (1978). Job burnout: How people cope. *Public Welfare, 36*, 56-58.

Maurer, A. (1979). Spare the child. *Journal of Clinical Child Psychology, 2*(3), 4-6.

Mayer, J., & Black, R. (1977). Child abuse and neglect in families with an alcohol or opiate addicted parent. *Child Abuse and Neglect, 1*(1), 85-98.

McCarthy, B. J., Rochat, R. W., Cundiff, B., Gould, P. A., & Quave, S. (1981a). Child abuse registry in Georgia: Three years of experience. *Southern Medical Journal, 74*(1), 11-16.

McCarthy, J., & Radish, E. S. (1983). Education and child bearing among teen-agers. In E. R. McAnarney (Ed.), *Premature adolescent pregnancy and parenthood*. New York: Grune and Stratton.

McCord, J. (1983). A forty year perspective on effects of child abuse and neglect. *Child Abuse and Neglect, 7*, 265-270.

McCormack, A., Burgess, A. W., & Janus, M. D. (1986). Runaway youths and sexual victimization: Gender differences in an adolescent runaway population. *Child Abuse and Neglect, 10*(3), 387-395.

McFaddin, S. (1982). *Feelings and your body: A prevention curriculum for preschoolers*. Bellingham, Wash.: Coalition for Child Advocacy.

McGrath, J. E. (Ed). (1970). *Social and psychological factors in stress*. New York: Holt, Rinehart, and Winston.

McMaster University Department of Clinical Epidemiology and Biostatistics. (1981). How to read clinical journals: To learn about a diagnostic test. *Canadian Medical Association Journal, 124*, 703-710.

McNamee, A. S. (1982). *Children and stress: Helping children cope*. Washington: Association for Childhood Education International.

Mehta, M. N., Lokeshwar, M. R., Bhatt, S. S., Athavale, V. B.,& Kulkarni, B. S. (1979). Rape in children. *Child Abuse and Neglect, 3*(3-4), 671-677.

Meier, J. H. (1985). Definition, dynamics, and prevalence of assault against children: A multifactorial model. In J. H. Meier (Ed.), *Assault against children*. San Diego, Calif.: College-Hill Press.

Menzel, H. (1950). Comment on Robinson's 'ecological correlations and the behavior of individuals.' *American Sociological Review, 15*, 674.

Merrill, E. J. (1962). Physical abuse of children: An agency study. In V. de Francis (Ed.), *Protecting the battered child*. Denver: American Humane Association.

Middleton, J. L. (1984, September-October). Double stigma: sexual abuse within the alcoholic family. *Focus on Family*, pp. 6-10.

Mones, P. (1985). The relationship between child abuse and parricide. In E. H. Newberger & R. Bourne (Eds.), *Unhappy families*. Littleton, Mass.: PSG Publishing Co.

Monopolis, S., & Sarles, R. M. (1985). The impact of maltreatment on the developing child. In C. M. Mouzakitis & R. Varghese (Eds.), *Social work treatment with abused and neglected children*. Springfield, Ill.: Charles C. Thomas.

Morse, A. E., Hyde, J. N., Newberger, E. H., & Reed, R. B. (1977). Environmental correlates of pediatric social illness: Preventive implications of an advocacy approach. *American Journal of Public Health, 67*(7), 623-625.

Mouzakitis, C. M. (1984). Characteristics of abused adolescents and guidelines for intervention. *Child Welfare, 63*(2), 149-157.

Mueller, D. P., Edwards, D. W., & Yarvis, R. M. (1977). Stressful life events and psychiatric symptomatology: CHange or undesirability? *Journal of Health and Social Behavior, 18*, 307-327.

Myers, J., & Peters, W. D. (1987). *Child abuse reporting legislation in the 1980s*. Denver: American Humane Association.

Nachmias, D., & Nachmias, C. (1981). *Research methods in the social sciences*. New York: St. Martin's Press.

Nash, C. L., & West, D. J. (1985). Sexual molestation young girls: A retrospective survey. In D. J. West (Ed.), *Sexual victimization: Two recent researches into sex problems and their social effects*. Aldershot, England: Gower Publishing.

National Committee for Prevention of Child Abuse. (1989, April). *NCPCA memorandum*. Chicago: National Committee for Prevention of Child Abuse.

National Institute of Child Health and Human Development. (n.d.). *Adolescent pregnancy and childbearing--rates, trends, and research findings*. Washington: National Institute of Child Health and Human Development.

National Indian Child Abuse and Neglect Resource Center. (1980). *Working with abusive and neglectful Indian parents*. Tulsa, Okla.: National Indian Child Abuse and Neglect Resource Center.

Newberger, C. M., & Newberger, E. H. (1980). The etiology of child abuse. In N. S. Ellerstein (Ed.), *Child abuse and neglect: A medical reference*. Somerset, N.J.: John Wiley and Sons, Inc.

Nie, N. H., Hull, C. H., Jenkins, J. G., Steinbrenner, K., & Bent, D. H. (1975). *Statistical package for the social sciences*. New York: McGraw-Hill.

Oates, K. (1986). *Child abuse and neglect: What happens eventually?* New York: Brunner-Mazel Publishers.

O'Brien, J. D. (1987). The effects of incest on female adolescent development. *Journal of the American Academy of Psychoanalysis, 15*(1), 83-92.

O'Donnell, S. M., Franco, S. M., Andrews, B. F., O'Connor, C.(1982). Child abuse and neglect research. *Journal of the Kentucky Medical Association, 80*(11), 710-723.

Okeahialam, T. C. (1984). Child abuse in Nigeria. *Child Abuse and Neglect, 8*(1), 79-73.

Oliver, J. E. (1985). Successive generations of child maltreatment: Social and medical disorders in the parents. *British Journal of Psychiatry, 147*, 484-490.

Ostbloom, N., & Crase, S. J. (1980). A model for conceptualizing child abuse causation and intervention. *Social Casework, 61*(3), 164-172.

Parton, N. (1985). *The politics of child abuse*. New York: St. Martin's Press.

Passman, R. H., & Mulhern, R. K., Jr. (1977). Maternal punitiveness affected by situational stress: An experimental analogue of child abuse. *Journal of Abnormal Psychology, 86*(5), 565-569.

Paulsen, M. G. (1966). Legal protections against child abuse. *Children, 13*, 42-48.

Pavenstedt, E., & Bernard, V. W. (1971). *Crises of family disorganization: Programs to soften their impact on children*. New York: Behavioral Publications.

Pearlin, L. I., & Aneshensel, C. S. (1986). Coping and social supports. In L. H. Aiken & D. Mechanic (Eds.), *Applications of social science to clinical medicine and health policy*. New Brunswick, N. J.: Rutgers University Press.

Pearlin, L. I., Lieberman, M. A., Menaghan, E. G., & Mullan, J. (1981). The stress process. *Journal of Health and Social Behavior, 22*, 337-356.

Pelton, L. H. (1978). Child abuse and neglect: The myth of classlessness. *American Journal of Orthopsychiatry, 48*, 608-617.

Pelton, L. H. (1981). Child abuse and neglect: The myth of classlessness. In H. Pelton (Ed.), *The social context of child abuse and neglect*. New York: Human Sciences Press.

Perlman, R., & Gurin, A. (1972). *Community organization and social planning*. New York: John Wiley and Sons.

Philips, I. (1983). Opportunities for prevention in the practice of psychiatry. *American Journal of Psychiatry, 140*(4), 389-395.

Pierce, R. L. (1979). *A stress frustration aggression paradigm*. Doctoral dissertation.

Plotkin, R. C., Azar, S., Twentyman, C. T., & Perri, M. G. (1981). A critical evaluation of the research methodology employed in the investigation of causative factors of child abuse and neglect. *Child Abuse and Neglect, 5*, 449-455.

Polansky, N. A. (1971). Research in social work. *The encyclopedia of social work* (16th issue). Vol. II. New York: National Association of Social Workers.

Polier, J. W. (1979). Professional abuse of children: Responsibility for the delivery of services. In D. G. Gil (Ed.), *Child abuse and violence*. New York: Ams Press.

Presser, H. B. (1974). Early motherhood: Ignorance or bliss? *Family Planning Perspectives, 6*, 8-14.

Putnam, F. W., Guroff, J. J., Silberman, E. K., Barban, L., & Post, R. M. 1986). The clinical phenomenology of multiple personality disorder: Review of 100 recent cases. *Journal of Clinical Psychiatry, 47*(6), 285-293.

Putnam, N., & Stein, M. (1985). Self-inflicted injuries in childhood: A review and diagnostic approach. *Clinical Pediatrics, 24*(8), 514-518.

Quebec Ministry of Justice. (1984). *Child abuse: Even in Quebec*. Quebec: Quebec Ministry of Justice.

Rahe, R. H., & Arthur, R. J. (1978). Life change and illness studies: Past history and future directions. *Journal of Human Stress, 4*, 3-15.

Resnick, P. J. (1969). Murder of the newborn: A psychiatric review of neonaticide. *American Journal of Psychiatry, 126*, 1414-1420.

Ritchie, J., & Ritchie, J. (1981). Child rearing and child abuse: The Polynesian context. In J. E. Korbin (Ed.), *Child abuse and neglect: Cross-cultural perspectives*. Berkeley: University of California Press.

Roberts, M. C., & Maddux, J. E. (1982). A psychosocial conceptualization of nonorganic failure to thrive. *Journal of Clinical Child Psychology, 11*(3), 216-116.

Robinson, W. S. (1950). Ecological correlations and the behavior of individuals. *American Sociological Review, 15*, 351-357.

Rose, R. (1972). The market for policy indicators. In A. Shonfield & S. Shaw (Eds.), *Social indicators and social policy*. London: Social Science Research Council.

Rosenfeld, A. (1987). Freud, psychodynamics and incest. *Child Welfare*, 66(6), 485-496.

Ross, L. (1977). The intuitive psychologist and his shortcomings: Distortions in the attribution process. In L. Berkowitz (Ed.), *Advances in experimental social psychology*, Vol. 10. New York: Academic Press.

Runtz, M., & Briere, J. (1986). Adolescent acting-out and childhood history of sexual abuse. *Journal of Interpersonal Violence*, 1(3), 326-334.

Ruskin, S. E. (1984). Incest is ugly, not the victims! *Victimology*, 9(3-4), 308-312.

Salter, A. C., Richardson, C. M., & Kairys, S. W. (1985). Caring for abused preschoolers. *Child Welfare*, 64(4), 343-356.

Sandberg, D. N. (1986). *Chronic acting out students and public school interventions: A manual for educators*. Boston: Boston University School of Law.

Sattin, D. B., & Miller, J. K. (1971). The ecology of child abuse within a military community. *American Journal of Orthopsychiatry*, 41(4), 675-678.

Savells, J., & Bash, S. (1979). Child abuse and the nuclear family. *National Forum: The Phi Kappa Phi Journal*, 69(1), 41-43.

Schaffer, B., & DeBlassie, R. R. (1984). Adolescent prostitution. *Adolescence*, 19(75), 689-696.

Schecter, J. O., Schwartz, H. P., & Greenfield, O. G. (1987). Sexual assault and anorexia nervosa. *International Journal of Eating Disorders*, 6(2), 313-316.

Schene, P. (1984). Economic correlates of neglect. In D. C. Bross (Ed.), *Multidisciplinary advocacy for mistreated children*. Denver: National Association for Counsel for Children.

Scherzer, L. N., & Lala, P. (1980). Sexual offenses committed against children. *Clinical Pediatrics*, 19(10), 679.

Schilling, R. F., Kirkham, M. A., & Schinke, S. P. (1985). *Coping, social support, and the prevention of maltreatment of handicapped children*. Seattle: Washington University Child Development and Mental Retardation Center.

Schmale, A. H., & Iker, H. P. (1971). Hopelessness as a predictor of cervical cancer. *Social Science and Medicine*, 5, 95-100.

Schmidt, W. S. (1977). Incestuous behavior as an etiological factor leading to juvenile delinquency and crime. In *Child abuse: Where do we go from here?* Washington:Children's Hospital National Medical Center.

Selvin, H. C. (1965). Durkheim's suicide: Further thoughts on a methodological classic. In R. A. Nisbet (Ed.), *Emile Durkheim*. Englewood Cliffs, N. J.: Prentice-Hall.

Sills, J. A., Thomas, L. J., & Rosenbloom, L. (1977). Nonaccidental injury: A two-year study in central Liverpool. *Developmental Medicine and Child Neurology, 19*, 26-33.

Silver, L. B. (1968). Child abuse syndrome: A review. *Medical Times, 96*(8), 803-820.

Simkins, L. (1984). Consequences of teenage pregnancy and motherhood. *Adolescence, 19*, 39-54.

Sklar, J., & Berkov, B. (1974). Teenage family formation in postwar America. *Family Planning Perspectives, 6*, 80-90.

Skuse, D. (Extreme deprivation in early childhood - II: Theoretical issues and a comparative review. *Journal of Child Psychology and Psychiatry, 25*(4), 543-572.

Smith, S. M. (1975). *The battered child syndrome*. London: Butterworth.

Smith, S. M., & Caplan, H. (1980). Some aspects of violence in families. *International Journal of Family Psychiatry 1*(2): 153-166.

Smith, S. M., & Hanson, R. (1974). 134 battered children: A medical and psychological study. *British Medical Journal, 3*, 666-670.

Smith, S. M., Hanson, R., & Noble, S. (1974). Social aspects of the battered baby syndrome. *British Journal of Psychiatry, 125*, 568-582.

Snyder, J. C., Hampton, R., & Newberger, E. H. (1983). Family dysfunction: Violence, neglect, and sexual misuse. In M. D. Levin et al. (Eds.), *Developmental Behavioral Pediatrics*. Philadelphia: Saunders.

Sokol, R. (1976). *Some factors associated with child abuse potential.* 71st Annual Meeting of the American Sociological Association, New York.

Solnit, A. J. (1978). Child abuse: The problem. In J. M. Eekelaar & S. N. Katz (Eds.), *Family violence: An international disciplinary study*. Toronto: Butterworths.

Solomons, G. (1981). Child abuse and developmental disabilities. In *Proceedinsgs* In*Proceedings of the fifth national conference on child abuse and neglect*. Milwaukee: Region V Child Abuse and Neglect Resource Center.

Spearly, J. L., & Lauderdale, M. (1983). Community characteristics and ethnicity in the prediction of child maltreatment rates. *Child Abuse and Neglect, 7*(1), 91-105.

Srole, L., Langner, T. S., Michael, S. T., Opler, M. K., and Rennie, T. A. (1962). *Mental health in the metropolis: Midtown Manhattan study*. Vol. 1. New York: McGraw-Hill.

Starr, R. H. (1982). A research-based approach to the prediction of child abuse. In R. H. Starr (Ed.), *Child abuse prediction: Policy implications*. Cambridge, Mass.: Ballinger Publishing Co.

132

Steele, B. (1975). Working with abusive parents: A psychiatrist's view. *Children Today*, *4*, 3.

Steele, B. (1986). Notes on the lasting effects of early child abuse throughout the life cycle. *Child Abuse and Neglect*, *10*(3), 283-292.

Steele, B. (1987). Abuse and neglect in the earliest years: Groundwork for vulnerability. *Zero to Three*, *7*(4), 14-15.

Steele, B., & Pollock, C. B. (1968). Psychiatric study of parents who abuse infants and small children. In R. E. Helfer & C. H. Kempe (Eds.), *The battered child*. Chicago: University of Chicago Press.

Steinberg, L. D., Catalano, R., & Dooley, D. (1981). Economic antecedents of child abuse and neglect. *Child Development*, *52*(3), 975-985.

Steinmetz, S. K. (1980). Violence-prone families. *Annals of the New York Academy of Sciences*, *347*, 251-265.

Straus, M. A. (1978). *Family patterns and child abuse in a nationally representative American sample*. Child Abuse and Neglect Second International Congress, London.

Stother, D. B. (1986). Latchkey children: The fastest-growing special interest group in the schools. *Journal of School health*, *56*(1), 13-16.

Stuart, J., & Allen, L. (1984). Incest: You too?! *Victimology*,*9*(3-4), 312-316.

Subramanian, K. (1985). Reducing child abuse through respite center intervention. *Child Welfare*, *64*(5), 501-509.

Sudia, C. E. (1981). What services do abusive and neglecting families need? In L. H. Pelton (Ed.), *The social context of child abuse and neglect*. New York: Human Sciences Press.

Sudman, S., & Bradburn, N. M. *Asking questions*. San Francisco: Jossey-Bass Publishers.

Suls, J., & Mullen B. (1981). Life events, perceived control and illness: The role of uncertainty. *Journal of Human Stress*, *7*, 30-34.

Summit, R. (1985). Causes, consequences, treatment, and prevention of sexual assault against children. In J. H. Meier (Ed.), *Assault against children: Why it happens - how to stop it*. San Diego: College-Hill Press.

Sutherland, D. (1976). Color me gray: Part II. *Social and Rehabilitation Record*, *3*(1), 8-11.

Tardieu, A. (1860). Etude medico-legale sur les services et mauvais traitements exerces sur des enfants. *Annales d'Hygiene Publique et Medecine Legale*, *13*, 361-398.

Thomas, J. N., & Rogers, C. M. (1984). Behavioral changes and parental responses in cases of child sexual molestation from an urban pediatric hospital. *Clinical Proceedings*, CHNMC, *40*, 222-229.

Timasheff, N. S. (1967). *Sociological theory*. New York: Random House.

Tong, L., Oates, K., & McDowell, M. (1987). Personality development following sexual abuse. *Child Abuse and Neglect, 11*(3), 371-383.

Trube-Becker, E. (1977). The death of children following negligence: Social aspects. *Forensic Science, 9*(2), 111-115.

Turner, J. H. (1982). *The structure of sociological theory*. Homewood, Illinois: The Dorsey Press.

Tutzayer, F. A. (1984). A catastrophe theory model of child abuse. *Journal of Family Issues, 5*(3), 321-342.

U.S. Bureau of the Census. *Census of population and housing, 1980: Public-use microdata samples technical documentation.* Washington: U.S. Bureau of the Census.

U.S. Bureau of the Census. *1983. Statistical abstract of the United States: 1981.* Washington: U.S. Bureau of the Census.

U.S. Dept. of Health and Human Services. (1980). *The American family at home and at work.* Washington: National Center on Child Abuse and Neglect, Children's Bureau, Administration for Children, Youth and Families, Office of Human Development Services, DHHS Publication (OHDS).

U.S. Dept. of Health and Human Services. (1987). *Young unwed fathers: Research review, policy dilemmas and options*. Washington: Department of Health and Human Services.

U.S. Dept. of Health and Human Services. (1988). *Study findings: Study of national incidence and prevalence of child abuse and neglect: 1988.* Washington: National Center on Child Abuse and Neglect, Children's Bureau, Administration for Children, Youth and Families, Office of Human Development Services, DHHS Publication (OHDS).

Usdan, M. D. (1978). The future of training-education for the prevention of child abuse and neglect. In M. L. Lauderdale, R. N. Anderson, & S. E. Cramer (Eds.), *Child abuse and neglect: Issues on innovation and implementation.* Washington: National Center on Child Abuse and Neglect.

van Rees, R. (1978). Five years of child abuse as a symptom of family problems. In J. M. Eekelaar & S. N. Katz (Eds.), *Family violence.* Toronto: Butterworths.

Vesterdal, J. (1981). Etiological factors and long-term consequences. In *Criminological aspects of the ill-treatment of children in the family.* Fourth Criminological Colloquium. Strasbourg, France: Council of Europe.

Vine, M. (1969). *An introduction to sociological theory.* New York: David McKay Co.

Walters, R. (1986). New Mexico State University child pornography. *Journal of Behavior Technology Methods and Therapy, 32*(1), 31-35.

134

Warren, D. I. (1980). Support systems in different types of neighborhoods. In J. Garbarino & H. Stocking (Eds.), *Protecting children from abuse and neglect*. San Francisco: Jossey-Bass Publishers.

Weaver, E. T. (1976). Child protection--a service concept and system. In *Fifth National Symposium on Child Abuse*. Denver: American Humane Association.

Weltz, A. (1984). *Bay area crisis nursery*. Prepared statement for Select House Committee on Children, Youth, and Families, San Francisco.

Wethers, D. (1978). Child abuse and neglect. *New York State Journal of Medicine, 78*(4), 610-611.

White, R. B., & Cornely, D. A. (1981). Navajo child abuse and neglect study: A comparison group examination of abuse and neglect of Navajo children. *Child Abuse and Neglect, 5*(1), 9-17.

Whiting-O'Keefe, Q. (1984). Choosing the correct unit of analysis in medical care experiments. *Medical Care, 22*, 1101-1114.

Wight, B. W. (1969). The control of child-environment interaction: A conceptual approach to accident occurrence. *Pediatrics, 44*, 799-805.

Wilbur, C. B. (1984). *The effect of child abuse on psyche*. Symposium on Childhood Antecedents of Multiple Personalities.

Winestone, M. C. (1985). Compulsive shopping as a derivative of a childhood seduction. *Psychoanalytic Quarterly, 54*(1), 70-72.

Wolfgang, M. E. (1982). Family stress and child abuse. In A. S. McNamee (Ed.), *Children and stress: Helping children cope*. Washington: Association for Childhood Education International.

Yeatman, A. E. (1980). Children and coercive parental authority: Towards a sociological perspective. In J. A. Scutt (Ed.), *Violence in the family*. Canberra, Australia: Australian Institute of Criminology.

Young, M. (1984). Counterphobic behavior in multiple molested children. *Child Welfare, 63*(4), 333-339.

Zalba, S. R. (1967). The abused child: II, a typology for classification and treatment. *Social Work, 12*, 70-79.

Zelnick, M., & Kantner, J. F. (1978). Contraceptive patterns and premarital pregnancy among women aged 15-19 in 1976. *Family Planning Perspectives, 10*, 135-142.

Zetterberg, H. L. (1966). *On theory and verification in sociology*. Totowa, N. J.: Bedminster Press.

Index

136